Black Belt Mind

OVERCOMING ANXIETY, DEPRESSION AND
ANTIDEPRESSANTS

David H. Fox

Phoenix Rising Publishers

Also available by David Fox:

Change your Life! Hope and Healing for Anxiety and Depression

Change Your Life! covers some of the most useful and proven techniques in psychology today including cognitive behavioural therapy, acceptance and commitment therapy, meditation and mindfulness which are all incredibly effective and proven in helping people who are anxious or depressed, or even for those who simply want to feel better about themselves and their lives. In this book you will learn how to regain control of your emotions and your life in a sustainable and practical way.

Change your Life! will provide you with tools and techniques that you can immediately put into action, including how to: challenge your negative and faulty thinking; think about and use the benefits of exercise; do simple meditation and why it is so effective; cope with change and negative emotions; remember to praise yourself; develop meaningful and powerful goals; keep yourself focused and stay committed to your new way of life!

Customer Reviews from Amazon:
"I found this book to have very useful tips on how to cope with and cure oneself from anxiety and depression"– C. Meyer

"David fox is a gifted writer... I loved this book. I liked that it has true life experience behind it!! Looking forward to his next. "– D. Olsen

Copyright © 2018 by David Fox.

All rights reserved. No part of this publication may be reproduced, distributed or transmitted in any form or by any means, including photocopying, recording, or other electronic or mechanical methods, without the prior written permission of the publisher, except in the case of brief quotations embodied in critical reviews and certain other noncommercial uses permitted by copyright law. For permission requests, write to the publisher, addressed "Attention: Permissions Coordinator," at the address below.

This publication contains the opinions and ideas of its author. It is intended to provide helpful and informative material on the subjects addressed in the publication. It is sold with the understanding that the author and publisher are not engaged in rendering medical, health, or any other kind of personal professional services in the book. The reader should consult his or her medical, health, or other competent professional before adopting any of the suggestions in this book or drawing inferences from it. The author and publisher specifically disclaim all responsibility for any liability, loss, or risk, personal or otherwise, which is incurred as a consequence, directly or indirectly, of the use and application of any of the contents of this book.

Phoenix Rising Publishers
521 Gardeners Road, Rosebery
Rosebery, New South Wales 2031

Ordering Information:

Quantity sales. Special discounts are available on quantity purchases by corporations, associations, and others. For details, contact info@foxpsychology.com.au

Black Belt Mind/ Fox, David. —1st ed.

ISBN 978-0-6483477-1-2

David Fox

DISCLAIMER

This book does not provide medical advice. If you would like medical advice please see a doctor or psychiatrist. If you would like insight and the tools that may assist you in overcoming anxiety, depression and anti-depressant medications then you may want to consider what I have to say in the following pages. However, just as the videos say, "Do not try this at home," especially by yourself. Make sure you have the RIGHT kind of support, which may include a counsellor who understands the ins and outs of anxiety and depression and the benefits and drawbacks of anti-depressant medications.

Please note: Do not abruptly stop most psychiatric drugs! Most psychiatric drugs are far more dangerous to take than people realize, but they also can become dangerous when discontinued too abruptly. Most have addictive qualities and can produce withdrawal symptoms that are emotionally and physically distressing and sometimes life-threatening. Stopping psychiatric drugs should usually be done gradually, and only with professional guidance.

A further note: This publication contains the opinions and ideas of its author. It is intended to provide helpful and informative material on the subjects addressed in the publication. It is sold with the understanding that the author and publisher are not engaged in rendering medical, health, or any other kind of personal professional services in the book. The reader should consult his or her medical, health, or other competent professional before adopting any of the suggestions in this book or drawing inferences from it. The author and publisher specifically disclaim all responsibility for any liability, loss, or risk, personal or otherwise, which is incurred as a consequence, directly or indirectly, of the use and application of any of the contents of this book.

Contents

INTRODUCTION 1
THE TRAPS OF ANXIETY, DEPRESSION AND ANTI-DEPRESSANTS 13
CHANGING YOUR BELIEFS 55
SELF-DISCIPLINE: A CRITICAL KEY TO BEATING ANXIETY AND DEPRESSION 69
IT'S ALL ABOUT ENERGY 81
FOOD FOR THOUGHT 93
RUN FOR YOUR LIFE 115
MEDITATION IS MANDATORY 129
SCIENCE VERSUS SPIRIT 141
FINDING YOUR PASSION AGAIN 151
WHAT YOU RESIST WILL PERSIST 157
YOU ARE NOT WHO YOU THINK YOU ARE… 165
QUESTION EVERYTHING…AND EVERYONE 173
HOPE: THE LAST BASTION OF THE HUMAN SPIRIT 179
WARNING: THE SIDE EFFECTS OF BEING OFF ANTIDEPRESSANTS 185
FURTHER READING 193
ABOUT THE AUTHOR 195

Acknowledgements

For Rael, Barry, Wendy, Susie, Michael and Leah, who were there for me...some miraculously and by divine providence I am sure... and then to my parents and sisters who have been there through some very difficult times.
Thank you all.

For my children Jake, Brandon and Lily – you mean the world and the universe to me.
I am so delighted to be your father.
Whilst it is in part because of me that you are here, it is very much because of you that I am here.

In memoriam:

For my aunty Linda Green Steinberg. You were such an example of light and love for me and countless others. Your warm heart and home knew no bounds.
May we all strive to be as loving, thoughtful and generous in spirit as you

Dedication

*I stand here before you on the shoulders of giants.
If I have achieved any modicum of wisdom and
understanding on this earth about the human condition and
the capacity for human achievement, success, joy, health and
happiness, it is because of those who have gone before.*

*Those who have lit the path of discovery for all of us still
searching in this dark, sometimes frightening journey to
discover who we truly are and how much love we have inside
and how capable we are of elevating ourselves and thereby
elevating all those we come into contact with.*

*To Louise Hay – who taught us the power of self-compassion
to heal not only our hearts but our minds, bodies and souls.*

*To Normal Vincent Peale – who urged us to change our
thinking by a conscious endeavor and reap the benefits of a
positive life.*

*To Dr. Wayne Dyer – who taught us that there truly is a
spiritual solution to every problem. I cannot thank you
enough for synchronistically coming back into my life when
you did and lifting me up when I had fallen.*

*To Tony Robbins – who taught us that success leaves clues
and that if we endeavor to live a passionate life, we can
achieve anything we set our minds to.*

To Esther and Jerry Hicks – who showed us that even if people may think we're off with the fairies, we can connect with infinite intelligence and share our spirituality with all those who so desperately need our help, and that there is only love, joy and growth.

And to Marshall Mathers (Eminem) – who has from the very beginning showed unbelievable courage in sharing his life, his struggles and his humanity with the world.

And to all those in the self-help genre who give of themselves every day so that we can live the best possible lives, full of peace, joy, health, wealth, happiness and success.

I salute you all.

David Fox
Sydney, Australia
1st of December, 2018

Introduction

"The two most important days in your life are the day you are born and the day you find out why"

-Mark Twain

Mastering the mind is something that we as human beings have been trying to do since the beginning of time. Poets, philosophers, mystics, scientists, psychologists and artists of all kinds have spent years of their lives trying to understand what makes a human being tick. What is it that drives our motivations, achievements, successes, failures or our health, disease, and destructiveness? Even more importantly, what creates hope in human beings even in some of the direst situations that they may find themselves in? What creates the will to survive and continue going in the face of all opposition? Further, what exactly is the reason that we are here in the first place? Is life one big random accident or one huge and wonderful orchestra of constant unfolding towards higher and higher levels of love and consciousness? The answer to this last question is likely to divide almost any group of people who dare to discuss it.

As wonderful and interesting as these questions are to contemplate, they pale in comparison to the questions I am asking in this book about what it means to even be *human*.

For example, what happens to the human mind, body and spirit when covered in a sea of manmade chemicals which are wreaking havoc with their ability to function as was intended by the universal intelligence that created them and brought them into the world on the day they were born? What happens when these people can no longer trust their own thoughts or emotions because they don't know if what they are thinking or feeling is real or driven by the interference of a chemical substance which has never been proven to create positive psychological or health outcomes over time? What happens to these poor souls who have been told and now believe that the drugs they are taking are as necessary to their survival as insulin is to a diabetic without ever having been tested for a deficiency which could have caused their ailment in the first place?

Something seems to have gone horribly wrong in the middle of the 20th century in the search for a "magic bullet" for mental health and the quest to help and heal the human psyche and spirit. The thing that has gone wrong was the introduction of a medical model of the mind, which included the need to "diagnose" and classify people in order to provide psychiatric medications to change their brains and their minds.

People are told in no uncertain terms (by those who have been trained in the medical model of human psychology, which completely discounts the human spirit or our human ability to rise above just about any difficulty) that they must rely on a dangerous drug to correct the problems they are experiencing in their lives. Very few realise just how dangerous a flippant comment such as this from their doctor or anyone else really is.

One of the very real and concerning issues with these medications is that they can actually lead to incredible damage and even destruction of the very faculties that people need in order to overcome what is troubling them in their lives in the first place and return to the state of happiness, love and joy which is their natural birthright.

There are an ever-growing number of people who are hurting and struggling right across the world as we see an increasing number of people experiencing anxiety and depression in any given year. Statistics tend to be very similar across the Western world, with most estimates being that one in every ten people struggles with depression and one in every four to five people struggles with anxiety of some kind.

A World Health Organisation (WHO) study recently provided statistics estimating that 4.4% of the world's population now suffer with depression, which equates to over 300 million people. Unfortunately, and quite tragically, these numbers are not lowering over time, even as the number of people being prescribed anti-depressant "medications" continues to skyrocket.

In Australia alone, the number of scripts for these medications has been increasing steadily. General practitioners (primary healthcare doctors) are writing scripts for anti-depressants totalling **30 million scripts** or more per year. Psychiatrists, on the whole, seem to be writing scripts for more or less the same amounts over the same time period which is around five million scripts per year. [1]

People are suffering and many are looking for better and safer ways to relieve their suffering. Many are looking to alternative practices, alternative healing and even spirituality to help them overcome not only their anxiety and depression but now also their addiction to the drugs that were meant to be helping them.

Although we are finally seeing the results of some longitudinal studies of these drugs – some thirty years after the release of the "wonder drug" Prozac – we still do not really know what the long term or even lifelong (in some cases) impact is of people being on these medications.

People are told that they need these drugs like a "diabetic needs insulin". This has been used as a standard mantra by the medical fraternity to get people to continue to take the drugs, even when they are suffering with side effects that are so debilitating they are losing their jobs, their families, their mental and physical health and saddest of all, their own connection to what it means to be a human being.

---

[1] Australian Department of Health (2012-2016).

I say the latter because what are we if we cannot experience our own thoughts and true emotions anymore? What is this life all about if we cannot truly experience love, sadness, hope, despair, joy, exhilaration, devastation, excitement, sexual arousal, connection, and motivation? All these things can be and usually are taken away, or at least severely muted, for those who are given these drugs.

CAVEAT: These drugs MAY BE appropriate when someone is severely depressed and incapacitated by anxiety or depression. This would be when they cannot get out of bed, function in their lives, connect to their loved ones or earn a living and where they may also be actively suicidal. It is in those cases that there MAY be cause to prescribe antidepressants.

However, this should only be done in conjunction with a team of professionals, including a doctor and a counsellor. Nobody can recover from anxiety or depression over the long term without talking to someone who can assist them in figuring out what is causing the anxiety or depression in the first place. Counsellors should work with their clients to teach them new ways to relate to their world, perceive the life experiences that they have had and help them put these into a context and meaning that is no longer disturbing or traumatic to them.

Clients should be provided with the tools that they need to build their life resiliency skill set so that they can put into place these skills and tools to ride the inevitable storms of life in a much safer and ultimately life-giving and life-growing manner.

It is an interesting question to try to uncover the cause of so much ongoing and increasing anxiety and depression in the world. And while there are no easy or simplistic answers to this ... there ARE solutions. There are many solutions that do not involve the very high risk of making people much worse through medication and where there is a risk that they could possibly lose themselves and their lives altogether. Hundreds and thousands of people's lives have been severely impacted through broken relationships, broken careers, broken families and suffering tremendous loss to their health, wellbeing and quality of life.

Unfortunately, I know about this very intimately; I felt like that a few years ago. However, there *is* hope and healing for those whose lives have been deeply affected by anxiety, depression and being caught up in the nightmare of antidepressant withdrawal syndrome.

In October 2013, I published an article on a website run by the award-winning investigative journalist Robert Whitaker. That article, which described my own struggle with medications over the prior 13 years, hit a chord with people from all age groups, all ethnicities, and all religious backgrounds right across the world.

Within two years, over 100,000 people had read the article. As a result of that I received hundreds of emails from people who were desperate to heal themselves and change their lives for the better. They would all tell a similar story of their agony, anguish and frustration at not being able to withdraw themselves (or in some cases their loved ones) from these terribly addictive drugs which the pharmaceutical companies STILL deny are addictive in any way. There is now even controversy over what the word "addiction" means as people try to define it as a physical versus mental and emotional phenomenon in order to separate the issue and in an attempt once again to downplay it. The facts, however, about the terrible impact these drugs are having are revealed by the hundreds and thousands of people who are stuck on these drugs who discuss their stories, their dismay, and their fear of never getting their lives back in online chat and support forums.

And while the doctors, psychiatrists, professors and other "experts" debate whether antidepressant withdrawal is real or not, the people living through this awful nightmare continue to suffer with no end in sight.

The pharmaceutical companies have only conceded to call the issue "antidepressant discontinuation syndrome". They can call it whatever they want; it is a very real and pressing global issue. Billions of dollars are being made by the pharmaceutical companies, while psychiatrists charge exorbitant prices for their "services", which are government subsidised, and counselling and psychological services are seen as a lesser need and clients are only given a meagre rebate and only a maximum of ten sessions per year (in Australia).

As one author put it, there is an "unprecedented global mass experiment happening on humanity" and it is high time more people raised the alarm bells. It has to stop before any more adults and an increasing number of teenagers take their lives. Yes, there are hundreds of teenagers committing suicide as a *direct result* of being prescribed antidepressant drugs every day. And that is with publicly available warnings that antidepressants are known to cause suicidal ideation in teenagers.

Eight people die by suicide in Australia every single day (Aventis-Beyond Blue study, 2014). Some may not be able to be saved, but most probably can. These people need hope; they need love; they need someone to talk to who actually listens to them and who cares enough about them to find out *why* they are unhappy, anxious, sad, or depressed. What they *don't need* is a doctor or psychiatrist listening to them with half an ear, and then "diagnosing" them with some kind of *"mental illness"* which *requires* drugging their brains.

The chemical imbalance theory of depression has never been proven, as award winning investigative journalist Robert Whitaker explained in his seminal and best-selling book *Anatomy of an Epidemic*. We have only ever suspected that lowered levels of serotonin are the cause of major depression. There are many ways to train the body to increase serotonin naturally, proven by research, including cardiovascular exercise, meditation, and a diet which includes a range of green leafy vegetables, vitamins, amino acids and omega 3 fish oils.

In addition, counselling - including cognitive behaviour therapy (CBT) – plays a critical role in helping those who are struggling with their mental health. In fact, time and time again research studies have shown that experiments comparing drugs with cognitive behaviour therapy indicate CBT is as effective as the drugs – with no side effects and greater long-term recovery. Additional research studies have shown that placebo groups often do as well as if not much better over the short and long term than the drug groups.

What proof do we have that those who are depressed actually have a physical (i.e., tested through some kind of medical test) deficiency of serotonin? There are no current tests that I know of that are being run in doctor's or psychiatrist's offices that prove that the person sitting in the chair across from them has *any* such deficiency in their brain or their body. And even if they did, why would dangerous drugs be the first port of call?

The patient sits there crying their eyes out because their husband or wife left them, or because they are in desperate financial difficulty, or because they lost a parent, or because they just had a baby and it turned their entire world upside down and the question foremost in the doctor's mind should be...what does that person *need*? Does he or she really **need** drugs? Is a mind-altering and dangerous drug really the answer? There is more than enough proof of adverse side effects listed on every major reporting system as well as the countless accounts online in support group forums.

If they don't need drugs, and most people with anxiety or depression probably don't, then what will help them get better? What do anxious or depressed people really need?

They need love, they need compassion, and they need friends and family who care about them, or at least someone in the helping professions who does. They may need some new ways of thinking and being in the world. They may need to look at their diet and exercise regimens. They may need to start making some difficult life choices about who they allow to be around them. They may need to change the direction of their careers and start doing something more meaningful to them. They may need to leave that marriage or relationship that is tearing them apart and distorting their concept of who they really are, as was the case with me.

What they don't need is to be given highly dubious drugs that do not follow the first principle of the Hippocratic oath that every single doctor, psychiatrist or other helping professional should abide by, which is simply that they should...

"FIRST, DO NO HARM."

Unfortunately, that is not the case when it comes to the psychiatric drugs and if anyone knows the truth about that statement, it is me.

And that is why NOW is the time for this message, this book and this revolution in mental health care.

As the saying goes, "There is nothing more powerful than an idea whose time has come." And I am certainly not the only person in the world who is raising the alarm about the detriment and damage that these drugs are doing to people's lives.

Through this book I have a story of hope and triumph to share with the world to let people know that there is another way.

I can only hope enough people get to read the message of hope in this book and act before they too have to go down the road that I had to go down. There is NOTHING more important to me than that this book becomes a guiding light - which I never had the opportunity to have - for people *before* they decide whether they really need to take an antidepressant.

Not one "professional" ever told me the upside and the downside of these awful drugs – most likely because they just didn't know themselves. They only knew what they had been taught in their psychiatry textbooks and then what the drug companies had marketed to them.

I would NEVER have been willing to take the chance had I had any inkling that I might never have been able to come off them, even when the crisis had passed. These drugs took 17 years of my life, but in the end, they also gave me something infinitely greater…the training in how to develop *a black belt mind*.

I have been fully schooled, trained, disciplined, terrorised, humiliated, judged, doubted, and put down due to these heinous drugs, but I was never totally beaten by them because my spirit was and remains infinitely more powerful than any drug or any other human being's opinion of who I am or what I can be, do or have.

My desire to keep going, to prove to myself and the world that I didn't need them and that in fact, I never needed them has been a driving force in my life for the past 17 years. The drugs won many battles with me over the course of those 17 years, but they never won the war. They came damn close but they NEVER won. And now, I have won the war.

It took absolutely every fiber of my being and everything that I had in me to keep looking for the answers, to keep refusing to be labelled and to keep getting up to face the responsibilities of my life while being crushed by debilitating anxiety and depression.

When I think back on it now, I don't know how I actually remained standing. My life during the last several years has included being a single father to two little boys and a baby girl for a few days every single week and working as a contract counsellor for not much pay and seeing around thirty people a week with some unbelievably intense situations and life events, including grief, separation, divorce, panic, anxiety, financial stress and traumatic incidents. Being somehow still able to contain all of that and keep going is something I perhaps do not give myself enough credit for.

I continued to not only work full time and see that huge volume of clients every single week but I also got into – because of my passion, of course – corporate training around anxiety, depression and mental health awareness for employees and managers. I did this because it was so close to my heart and I felt and still do feel very passionate about the need to remove the stigma and help people not suffer in silence like I did.

I have always had a passion for training others and facilitating discussions with groups around mental health and resilience and I love making a difference, even though there were many times where I was completely terrified that someone would notice what was going on with me. I am so thankful that is no longer a part of my life and that I can now run training sessions with only the usual jitters that any other presenter might experience.

Through this book as well as my website and social media, I will be sharing the insights and discoveries that I experienced along the journey and which I used to help me turn it all around.

In this book I will share with you what I have learned in my 24 years of searching for the answers on how to beat anxiety and depression. I count myself very lucky to have been able to last as long as I did and to have been able to change my life, get off the antidepressants and reclaim my mind, body, relationships with the people I love and care about as well as my career, my health and happiness.

More importantly, I have found my way back to me—the person I was before this all began. Not only have I found that person again but I have found an infinitely wiser, more empathic and appreciative human being who feels blessed to have another chance where my future is open and unlimited, where no one besides me gets to say who I am, what I can do, where I can go, who I can be with and what I can contribute to the world.

If you're wondering how I eventually overcame anxiety, depression and antidepressant drugs, the most important part of my answer is that I simply REFUSED to give up.

I stood up every time I got knocked down. I kept pushing even when I got to the point of thinking about ending it all. If you have ever experienced thoughts like that, you will know just how scary it is to think that leaving this world is somehow better for you and those around you than continuing the way you are. And so...

I REFUSED to give in to the opinions of every doctor, psychiatrist, psychologist, or family member who believed that I needed to be on these drugs "like a diabetic needs to be on insulin".

I REFUSED to believe that there was anything wrong with me aside from some very difficult and stressful life experiences that I knew I could resolve and overcome with the right support, tools, counselling, encouragement, spiritual guidance, discipline, meditation, exercise and lifestyle.

I REFUSED to believe - when I was knocked down and it seemed that things went from bad to worse - that the solution was to continue to increase the medication because "my" anxiety and depression were coming back. Tragically, this is something that nearly every doctor will tell their patients who have tried and failed to come off the drugs.

For those people who have been through some of what I have described above, for any of their friends or family members who have suffered alongside them, and for those who are looking for some hope that they can indeed take their lives back and be happy and fulfilled again, this book is for you.

Throughout the book, I will provide anecdotes from my own life experiences, which I have chosen to share with you because they were often hard-won and if they can help you save time, pain and difficulty on your own journey, I will be delighted.

However, this book is not just about my own life. It is a book that includes everything I have learned through being a psychologist, coach and counsellor to hundreds of people in eighteen years of my adult working life. Each of my clients shared with me some of their greatest challenges and most painful life experiences, and I am just so pleased to have been instrumental in helping them to find the tools, the insights, the awareness and the desire to do the work, make the changes, process the emotions and change their lives for the better.

This book is, of course, mostly about overcoming anxiety, depression and anti-depressants and has been written with the "soul" purpose of reaching out to YOU and sending a message of hope and recovery if you are battling with anxiety and depression that life doesn't have to be that way and your life and most importantly your future is not set in stone. You can change it. I am proof and so are the hundreds of clients I work with.

This is not a book about quick fixes, but that doesn't mean that it is not a very practical book that you can dip into at any time and find a chapter that resonates with what you are struggling with in that moment and what you need at a particular time on your journey to healing.

This book is unique in the self-help industry because it is written by a psychologist who speaks with KNOWLEDGE (not a belief or some theoretical understanding) of what it is like to experience anxiety and depression, as well as what it can be like to be stuck on antidepressants.

It is also a book about keeping the faith when everyone else is telling you that you're wrong and that you're being ridiculous thinking that you can change something which is biological in nature.

If only one life is saved because of the message and guidance I provide in this book, then all those years of hell will have been worth it.

I invite you to take your time with this book. Keep it nearby. Dip into one of the chapters that offers the support you need when you get stuck and use it as a constant reminder that you too can once again live your life free of anxiety, depression and antidepressant drugs.

CHAPTER ONE

The traps of anxiety, depression and anti-depressants

"The only thing we have to fear is fear itself."

– Franklin D. Roosevelt

Anxiety and depression are conditions of the human mind, body and spirit that are not well understood not only by those who struggle and suffer terribly with them but by those who are meant to be the "experts" in what they are and how best to treat them.

A person starts to find themselves not feeling like they usually have for most of their life and starts to experience a material and significant change to the quality and nature of their thoughts –from mostly optimistic and positive to negative, global and oppressive thinking that doesn't seem to let up. As their thinking begins to shift – at first possibly quite imperceptibly but over time much more obviously – towards thoughts of fear, sadness, regret, helplessness, hopelessness and ultimately, worthlessness, the person begins to notice some other changes occurring.

Some of these changes manifest in their physiology. They may start to notice that their heart races and they cannot really understand why. They may notice, in the case of anxiety, that they begin to sweat more profusely and without warning—a sudden onset of shallow breathing, tight chest, queasy stomach and, in some cases, vertigo and light-headedness.

When the person begins to experience these physical symptoms, the common practice is to look to physical causes. They may very well end up at the hospital hooked up to heart monitors and being checked for a heart attack. The symptoms of panic often mimic some of the warning signs that people have been told to look for in reference to having a heart attack. The thought that they may indeed be having a heart attack strikes fear and more anxiety into them and accelerates the very symptoms they have just begun to experience. This is one of the very first traps of anxiety...the initial physical response of the body to the fight-or-flight reaction, leading to the person becoming afraid of what is happening and, without the knowledge or understanding that nothing terribly bad can happen to them, they get completely overwhelmed with fear of what is happening in their own bodies.

Most people who struggle with major anxiety and depression think and feel that they cannot change what they are experiencing. One of the greatest dangers of someone experiencing major anxiety or depression is that they fall into these traps and conclude that they are stuck or lost forever in their pain. We know, in psychology, that it is those thoughts and feelings of helplessness, hopelessness and worthlessness that can lead people to pay the ultimate price for their pain. And as we all know, it is not just a price that they will pay but it is a price that everyone who knows and loves them will continue to pay forever.

And so, it is with this in mind that I will lay out in this first chapter my hard-won knowledge, understanding, and experience of these traps and the steps that can be taken to be released from each of these traps. If learned and understood by those who struggle with anxiety and depression, these steps can provide them with a range of ideas and tools to begin to lift the dark clouds of anxiety and depression from their minds, their bodies, their relationships and their lives.

The Traps of Anxiety

The first trap of anxiety: The fear of fear.

I will never forget the very first panic attack I had. It was in 1998 when a group of friends and I had gone to Cape Town, South Africa for a much-needed holiday. I was in my honours year of psychology and I was looking forward to getting out of Johannesburg and finally going to see what all the hype was about Cape Town, the second mother city of South Africa. My very close friend was an avid fisherman and decided that he would arrange for a few of the friends to go deep sea fishing. I was not interested in doing any such thing. I was quite happy to get myself off to the beach and check out all the tanned, bikini-clad females lounging around on their colourful towels. However, at the last minute one of the friends pulled out and my best friend begged me to join them because the cost was fairly high per person. I tried my best to explain that I would rather get my head stuck inside an oven than go deep sea fishing but he wasn't having a bar of it.

We were told not to eat any breakfast on the morning of the trip and so I remember waking up at 4:30am and taking a few bites of a granny smith apple.

We arrived at the wharf, a famous fishing wharf called – aptly enough – Fishhoek. We stood around in the morning cold and mist and looked at some of the boats that could have been possible candidates for our fishing charter and there was one we saw that was a double-decker, luxurious-looking boat with a huge cabin which sported a lounge, a large screen TV and what looked like a mini bar. I began to think this might not be so bad after all.

However, my excitement was very short-lived, as we heard someone shouting out to us who was passing by in what could only be described as a glorified dinghy with a motor attached to it. The two charter captains told us to follow them as they lowered the motorised surf board into the ocean. I remember saying something to my friend along the lines of "you have to be shitting me".

There were about five of us going on this jaunt plus the captain and his lacky, who seemed to me to be highly dodgy – especially considering how much they were charging for the privilege of putting our lives at risk far out to sea.

The boat had no seating area whatsoever, only a small hull the captain would steer the boat from and where one or two people could huddle if they wanted to get some cover from the elements.

So, with nowhere to sit, we all had to find a spot to stand and hold onto while the boat chugged out to sea.

Now, I need to explain a little something about the sea surrounding the lovely city of Cape Town. Even in the middle of summer, it is freezing cold. It is where the Indian Ocean meets the Atlantic Ocean. We used to go on most of our family holidays to the warmer waters of Durban, which is on the east coast of South Africa and smack bang in the middle of the Indian Ocean. Beautiful warm waters. Not so with Cape Town. Fish would jump onto the sand just to recover and then waddle back into the ocean after sunbathing long enough to brave the waters once more. Not really, but you get the point.

And that's assuming there were any fish near the water's edge at all which is highly doubtful, given the fact that in order for us to do the deep-sea fishing and have any remote chance of catching something, we needed to go two hours out to sea, directly away from the land. Two hours on a glorified tug boat, in drizzly cold weather, with the boat launching itself over and over each wave and then landing unceremoniously with a crash into the misty water.

I remember holding onto the railing just above the captain's spot for dear life whilst the spray from the sea and the ongoing drizzle from the cloudy morning ran down my shirt and completely soaked me from head to toe. I started to get very cold. And the farther out to sea we went, the fewer other life forms, boats and signs of any civilisation whatsoever we saw.

My mind started to rumble as I heard captain creepy pants talking on his radio to the other boats about the weather conditions and other seafaring issues I couldn't understand. I told my friend I wasn't feeling very well at all and he said not to worry and that it wouldn't be long before we found the fishing spot. After another few minutes, however, the boat seemed to cut out completely and we were just adrift in the ocean. On the one hand I was relieved that we weren't launching over waves anymore, but on the other hand we were now just drifting on the ocean and captain underpants then knelt down towards the back of the boat and started fiddling with the fuel line and muttering something to his co-idiot.

I started to picture us being stranded at sea, with no one close enough to us to reach us in time to save our souls from a watery death. Of course, that's a dramatic thought to have but in my 22-year-old mind, all I could see was how long the trip to this point had been, how far away from safety and land we were and how little food we had on board!

It was in that moment that my brain must have made an executive decision and the next thing I knew my entire body started reacting. I suddenly felt extremely cold. I felt a tingling sensation spread from my cheeks to my face and down to my arms and hands. I began to feel light-headed and thought – for some strange reason – that I was going into hypothermia. I suppose it was the only thing my young mind could come up with to explain what was going on in my brain and body. And as the tingling sensation and fear reached my hands I looked down and saw my fingers curl into what I can only describe as being a "claw-like" position and I fell to the ground. It was at this point that my friend and some of the others who had already been "feeding the fish" for the past hour or so became quite concerned about me.

My friend told the deep-sea militia that we should maybe turn around. They in turn looked at me in puzzlement and decided that it might be best to get closer to land again.

All I remember doing was looking out to sea with one of my other friends rubbing my back for warmth – no one knew what was happening to me – and as we got about half an hour away from land, the sun broke through the clouds and warmed us all up a bit. As I felt that warmth on my skin, I began to feel better and come out of it.

I had no idea what had hit me. To this day, all my friends who were on that trip still poke fun at me and laugh about what happened, even though when they do mention that trip they all get a look of mild terror in their eyes, and they were all as green as the ocean and mostly felt the pain of seasickness in a more classic way than I did.

It was only much later, when I was talking to a close female friend, when I described what happened that she said it could not have possibly been hypothermia and that she thought it may have been a panic attack.

I have only experienced that level of panic three times in my entire life and the last time it happened many years ago. The thing that ensured that it only lasted a minute or two and that I had no lingering struggle was because I knew exactly what it was and that it would run its course and be over soon enough. I now knew it couldn't do much to me aside from incapacitating my body for a minute or two and that, even at its worst, if I were to pass out from the irregular breathing, my autonomic nervous system would take over and ensure I continued to breathe normally until I regained consciousness.

Of course, this can be very scary for someone who is terrified of having a panic attack while driving or in a public place where they may hurt themselves quite severely and so I am in no way minimising the fear people have and the potential danger involved. However, what I am emphasising is that it is the initial shock of experiencing the brain and body taking over and putting us into a complete shutdown that is so unnerving to someone who has experienced a full-blown panic attack.

What I have described is probably one of the most extreme experiences one can have with anxiety. There is a scale of fear reactions in the body, from mild worry, stress and concern to the full-blown autonomic hijack I have described in my delightful deep-sea fishing tale.

And so, one of the first traps for people who experience anxiety is, then, the absolute fear of having to experience such a thing ever again and so any sign that a panic attack may be imminent can be the very thing that triggers and escalates the person's adrenal system to go into overdrive.

The key to subduing anxiety, then, is to normalise any symptoms that seem to be the oncoming of another panic attack. Shortness of breath, a racing heart, tightness in the chest—these can all be caused by a variety of other completely non-anxiety related reasons. Climbing up a flight of stairs when you're not particularly fit or even if you are could cause the anxious person to be triggered into thinking a panic attack is on the way and that thought in itself can bring a panic attack right on.

The anxious person has to learn to just observe what is happening in the body—not to disassociate but to observe and provide the emotional space for the body to do its thing without compounding the issue with panic and fear-driven thinking. This is a crucial key to overcoming panic.

The second trap of anxiety: Avoidance and procrastination

We all procrastinate to some degree in life; whether it is rearranging our messy cupboards, or rearranging our "messy" lives, we all do it. However, just because we do it doesn't mean that we *should* do it or that we should accept it. When it comes to managing and alleviating our stress and anxiety, one of the greatest traps in finding a way out of the stress and anxiety is the idea that if we ignore the issue it will go away. It is, of course, the old "ostrich with its head in the sand" analogy. An ostrich sees a heard of buffalo charging towards it in the distance and, in its fear of what it thinks is coming its way, puts its head in the sand, thinking that what it can't see anymore can't hurt it. It believes that this will solve the problem. It certainly allays the fear a little bit because it is no longer staring at that charging herd, paralysed with fear. And so it is with our worries and fears in life. When we get stuck in the throes of stress and anxiety, one of the common behavioural symptoms is quite often both procrastination and avoidance. We are afraid of something and we don't want to face it head-on.

I can attest to this, and this can relate to anything from doing one's taxes and fearing that one may owe the government a sum of money that would send one into bankruptcy and exacerbate our already-woeful financial situation right through to the fear that we may be losing our connection and attraction towards our partner and what that may entail for the future.

We may also avoid people at work, social get-togethers, exercise routines, important life tasks and an array of important and sometimes even critical tasks and responsibilities. Sometimes that thing that we are worried or fearful about becomes unmanageable or unsolvable in our minds and we do the ostrich thing, have that glass or bottle of wine, take the pill and send ourselves into oblivion...only to wake up the next day to face the stark reality that nothing has changed except our ability to wake up and face the day and get on with and do what we absolutely have to do to keep things afloat.

So, part of the solution for avoidance is clearly to tackle the problem. If we need some help, like just having a friend or other trusted person sitting in the room with us while we tidy up the mess and take some furtive steps towards resolving the thing causing us such deep distress, then we just need to do that. And then very often, and in most cases, we realise that the awful beasts we thought were about to eat us alive are only tamable zoo animals who just wanted our attention and for us to feed and pet them a little.

I fully appreciate the difficulties in getting yourself motivated or even facing for one second something that is causing you immense amounts of anxiety. However, I also know as much as you do that avoiding it is not the answer. Get help if you don't want to face it alone. Call a friend, see a counsellor, talk to a minister, talk to your boss, reach out for help because as soon as you make a dent in it...the fear levels will begin to shift and lower and as you sense headway and some progress you will build some momentum and it will get sorted. Fast. I promise. Just do it. Now. Put the book down or stop reading and do one little thing to make some progress and show anxiety, fear, procrastination and avoidance that they are NOT in control. YOU are in control.

The third trap of anxiety: Insert "Drug" of Choice or another suitable Band-Aid

When we are going through the throes of anything, from stress to anxiety or a full-blown panic attack, our first reaction is to want to flee from the painful physical, mental and emotional reactions of our minds and bodies. There is potentially nothing more debilitating to the human mind and body than to be crippled with fear – not only due to negative, irrational thoughts and fears about what may happen to us but in addition by the brain and body's physiological responses to that fear.

We get triggered by something—it doesn't really matter what the trigger is—and we have a very quick, automatic negative thought about it and our brain receives a signal that it/we are in danger. The brain does what it does best...it goes into survival mode and begins to shut down our prefrontal cortex, which is the home of our rational and creative thinking. We are filled with adrenalin and cortisol, which are designed to activate the body into fight-or-flight mode and help ensure that we survive this terrible onslaught that is about to engulf our very existence.

And so, quite understandably and with great compassion and empathy, I say the stressed, anxious or panicked soul turns to something...anything...that will help reduce the severity or the duration of the thoughts and feelings that are so uncomfortable. These "solutions" are ultimately either not very useful in reducing the feelings of anxiety or if they are, such as smoking, alcohol and/or other illicit drugs, they can lead to a dependence on them and a reduction in our ability to use our own God-given resources to move through our fears.

There are two traps hidden in this.

The first is what most people have been told and are fairly aware of when it comes to things like alcohol, illicit drugs and prescription drugs such as Xanax, Valium and other benzodiazepines. As we use these crutches more and more, their power and effect to lessen the anxiety becomes less and less. This is called habituation. And then we need to ingest more and more of these noxious products in order to feel the relief that we want and crave when the beast of anxiety rears its ugly head. Sometimes part of the process of weaning off the benzodiazepines is to just have one or two in your bag or wallet or somewhere else nearby, and the thought that it is there can sometimes allay the anxiety and help you to reverse the physiological activation that happens when anxiety begins to strike. Millions of people know the dangers of becoming used to and reliant on these products. We essentially become more and more disabled and the impact on our mental and physical health starts to become quite pronounced – not to mention the impact on our relationships with others around us.

If left unchecked, it can lead to the end of marriages and relationships, careers, parental privileges, friendships and even life itself. A very severe trap indeed. And unfortunately, we are always just masking the issue and trying to send ourselves into oblivion, which never seems to change the situation we are in for the better. Well, certainly not to my knowledge or in my professional experience with the hundreds of clients I have worked with over the years. These drugs are a Band-Aid solution – the type of Band-Aid which allows your wound to fester and ends up causing your finger to fall off. Not much point in the Band-Aid in that case. But it felt soothing when you put it over the wound, I am sure.

The second problem with using these drugs is that we start to become dependent on something outside of ourselves as the solution to our fear, anxiety and panic. Now, I will admit that I have used some of these options in the past – never illicit drugs, but certainly alcohol –and I have also taken Valium at various times to help quell the absolute horror that is rampant and what seems like unstoppable anxiety. However, what I described above was certainly my experience too. At one stage, the drugs just stopped working altogether and I realised I had to start relying more heavily on my other skills, such as meditative breathing, cardiovascular activity, cognitive behaviour therapy, as well as finding something infinitely more powerful than any drug...my own connection to the deepest part of me.

Sometimes it really takes facing our greatest and deepest fears head-on, with the attitude of the Vietnam vet in the Forest Gump movie who sat with no legs on the top mast of his boat in the middle of the wildest storm imaginable and shouted to the heavens to bring it on. We don't need to be fearless, just not afraid of fear itself.

Sometimes we just have to face the storm and take it on head-first, head up and let the sea of fear and anxiety crash down on us—and realise, when the sun breaks through the clouds and we open our eyes on the sandy beach and struggle to our feet again, that it may have knocked us down but it didn't knock us out. Not completely, not ever. Because it just doesn't have that kind of power and there is nothing ultimately more powerful than our human spirit and ability to get up again and again.

The fourth trap of anxiety: It keeps us safe

It may seem very strange to read what you just read above. Anxiety keeps us safe? Okay David, now you are contradicting yourself because you are saying that my anxiety is protective and keeps me safe but it's ruining my life and keeping me anything BUT safe by making me avoid the things I must do and messing up my body, my emotions, my focus, my productivity, my relationships and my health. How is it keeping me safe?!

Well, to answer that question we need to understand the very reason and purpose that fear and anxiety exist at all in our lives. What do you think that is? What possible reason would fear and anxiety have for being in our lives? You're getting something forming in your mind now, aren't you? To help us avoid danger.

If we didn't have the ability to perceive a threat to us in our environment, we would have perished very soon after we were born. Most of us wouldn't have made it past our first year of life if fear didn't serve a critical purpose...which is to warn us of the dangers up ahead and to keep us alive.

Now that is what we might call a "guidance system". If you were walking down the road and suddenly heard a screech of tires somewhere behind you and you turned around to see an out-of-control truck barreling down on you, your body would immediately react by shooting adrenalin and cortisol into your body to activate you to jump out of the way. It is the recognition by your brain of a danger that puts everything into motion and ends up saving your life, isn't it?

We can all pretty much relate to that example and we can see quite clearly that fear itself is purposeful and even helpful...sometimes. Not always, not even half the time. Maybe 10% of the time.

We might often experience mild to moderate levels of fear on a fairly regular basis but we don't even recognise or acknowledge to ourselves that that's what is happening. It takes a little self-reflection, ideally done using cognitive behaviour therapy tools to identify that this is what is happening within us and which thoughts in particular are in the driver's seat in those moments.

Moving away from the glaringly obvious danger of an out-of-control truck coming at you, let's see if there may be other fears that pop up for us during our day.

We fear that we won't get to work on time...we fear that we won't say the right thing in that job interview...we fear that the work we are doing is not up to scratch...we fear that someone is going to find out that we really don't know what we are doing at all and expose us...we fear that if we don't sterilise our baby's bottle that they will get terribly sick...we fear that she won't say yes if we ask her out on a date...we fear that he is just "mosting" – something new I learned from one of my female clients in counselling; it means that all the things he says about wanting everything we want are just a lie to get us into bed...we fear that we will make an absolute ass out of ourselves if we have to stand up and present in front of a crowd...we fear that we won't be liked anymore if we tell someone something that has been bothering us about the way they have been treating us (sometimes for years!)...we fear that we may never amount to anything...we fear that we are getting older and losing our looks and our youthful appearance...we fear that we may have married the wrong person...we fear leaving that job we hate because we may never get another one...we fear leaving an abusive relationship because we are safer staying where we are and copping the abuse...we fear going to visit a strange country where we may get lost and murdered or blown up...we fear a nuclear war starting between the USA and Korea...we fear Donald Trump accidentally tweeting the secret combination that launches a nuclear attack on Canada!

I could go on and on...and as much fun as that was to write and as curious as I am as to how many more I can come up with you may be reaching for your remote control so let us get to the point.

Our minds can very often run amok with endless imaginings and fears about what could happen in the future and it is only when we take these thoughts seriously that we can get really overwhelmed. This is also when we hold back and withdraw from life instead of stepping forward boldly and reaching for our grandest dreams.

So, let us once and for all, do our best to realise that we should never allow fear to rule our lives. We should understand that it has its purpose and reason for being a part of our human condition, which primarily is to keep us safe, but staying safe is not what we came to this earth to do. We came to explore, we came to contribute and we came to live in joy. So, let's move the fear aside and chase our dreams and our heart's greatest desires with abandon!

Let me clear here. I am not in any way minimising the debilitating struggle millions have with anxiety. I consider myself fully schooled and a veteran when it comes to anxiety but I also know that anxiety doesn't last and you CAN learn to tame it, if not eliminate it altogether. For other more specific tools such as exactly how cognitive behaviour therapy can assist with anxiety, you may want to check out my first book Change your Life: Hope and Healing for Anxiety and Depression.

The Traps of Depression

For those who have not experienced depression, it is very difficult to describe the mental torture and agony one goes through.

My first experience of depression was absolutely frightening. I just wanted to lie on the couch and sleep all day so that I could escape feeling like I was in black hole. I was embarrassed to see my friends and even felt that some of my family were judging me or thinking of me as "weak". The one thing I can say about the experience of depression is that unless you or someone you know has been through it, it's very hard to understand the torment of being locked up inside your own mind. It's hard to conceptualise how someone's world can become so dark and grey, with very little sense of meaning or purpose. It may be harder to understand why someone can't seem to get out of bed and get going or complete simple tasks like showering or eating! I lost a lot of weight during that time and at other times when I have experienced depression. I now know how common this symptom of depression is. I even had to take a meal supplement drink called "Ensure" because it was quick to make and easy to just drink down, hoping the vitamins and minerals would help my body get the nutrients it needed.

I suppose one could say that I have an intimate knowledge of depression and because I am someone with a forever curious and questioning mind, I have looked deeply at each element of depression and I have come to understand how it operates, what keeps it in place, what the traps of it are and therefore how you might avoid them or move through them.

The first trap of depression: Withdrawing from life

One of the biggest problems with depression is that the person going through it struggles so much with their own sense of self-worth that they become convinced people wouldn't want to be around them in the state they are in. And so, the natural thing to do is to withdraw from people, stop going out and meeting up with friends and family, and this only leads to greater feelings of isolation and worthlessness. The need for people who are depressed to stay connected to humanity is critical—however, only the RIGHT people. Only those who truly provide a non-judgmental space for the person struggling with depression to visit, engage and realise that life is still worth living because they may just find themselves smiling or laughing when they meet up with that friend or family member, and there is nothing more powerful to change the depressed person's mental funk than to realise that who they truly are still resides within them. And this often comes out when they engage with those they love and care about it and TRY to enjoy a little time outdoors, back in the world.

Other areas of withdrawal include a withdrawal from hobbies-passions, food, work and other vital activities which help stimulate positive thought and general wellbeing.

And so, it is clear that if you are struggling with depression, you absolutely have to fight with everything you have in you to stay engaged with life, with your friends, your family, your passions and the very stuff that makes life worth living. You need to find a way to connect again and not believe in the dark mirror that depression is trying to get you to believe in.

The second trap of depression: Lethargy

The depressed person experiences incredible lethargy of the mind and body. The trap here is that lethargy breeds more lethargy. The depressed person feels exhausted most of the time and due to this they tend to feel like they *need* to sleep. This leads them to sleep, of course, or lie down on the couch and as they spend more and more time doing this their energy continues to drop lower and lower. And then they feel even more tired, and so they won't go out and they certainly "can't exercise" because how could they possibly do anything energetic when they are so tired? So, you can see how this trap begins then and perpetuates itself unless something interrupts it.

It is very seductive to fall into this particular trap. It is certainly hard enough for most of us to muster up the energy to get up and exercise on a regular basis. Just ask anyone who has tried to lose weight or head to the gym at least a few times a week. Or ask someone who has struggled with a health concern and gone to the doctors and been told some dietary changes are in order. How easy is it to make those changes and keep them consistently so that they become a new way of life?

Finding the energy and motivation to make a change can be difficult for most people. When it comes to those who begin to fall into the traps of depression, it can seem like a complete impossibility. As depression begins to take hold, the person's energy levels begin to dip significantly. This may be due to them withdrawing from life, stopping their regular exercise routines, as well as potentially experiencing some significant drops in the levels of essential neurotransmitters, especially norepinephrine, which is the stimulatory neurotransmitter that elevates our energy levels.

With all of this going on, the person begins to feel more tired than usual and they start to struggle to get up in the mornings, feeling like they just don't have the energy. And so, they stay in bed or get up and force themselves to swallow something to eat and then head over to the couch to lie down. In this way, sleep becomes very alluring and attractive to the person who is falling into a depressed state. They are also plagued with negative thoughts which prevents them from getting up to face the world and so now body and mind are working against them.

It becomes preferable to the depressed person to not be here. Being asleep, they can escape the "reality" of their lives and the incredibly difficult and distressing negative thoughts and feelings that have begun to plague them on a daily basis. The hole deepens as they sleep more and as they sleep more the body does not generate enough energy of its own. The body can only generate energy and flow oxygen through the blood to all the vital parts of the body and brain through movement. As Einstein so wisely said, "nothing happens until something moves", and when nothing moves...no energy can be created.

Without movement, energy dissipates, becomes stale and the impact on the human mind and body can be quite devastating. We were clearly not made to be idle and sit still. In fact, very little on this earth is.

The nature of the world of work that we generally inhabit (aside from those work roles and careers that involve a lot of physical activity) means that we are sometimes not moving enough during each day. Without movement, we cannot generate the energy we need to stay healthy, vibrant, happy, and positive in thought. When it comes to depression, that can be multiplied a hundred-fold.

Research on high performers conducted by international high-performance expert Brendon Burchard has shown that those who are considered to be top performing right across the globe generate high levels of energy through ensuring they are active and moving their bodies through cardiovascular activity more than three times per week.

Research around the relationship between exercise, and in particular aerobic-cardiovascular exercise, has shown again and again that it is able to mitigate anxiety and depression. However, we also know that when someone falls into the traps of depression, there is often very little that will be able to get them up and go for a run or hit the gym. And so it becomes an incredible catch-22 situation.

A remedy for this is for the person suffering with depression to connect very strongly with the three W's. WHY do I want and need to exercise? WHO is going to suffer if I don't get up today and at least go for walk outside? WHAT is at stake if I do not find a way to take back my own power and reconnect my mind and body to my spirit? Sometimes it takes an almost herculean effort on the part of the depressed person to get up and just go and do anything, and this is what they most need to be encouraged to do by their loved ones and by themselves. It may not even take a hell of a lot for them to break the vicious cycle and turn it into a virtuous cycle of action leading to energy leading to positive thought, emotion, behaviour and so on.

And so, my greatest advice to you if you are struggling with this particular trap is GET UP and go and do something every single day – preferable in the morning because that is when depression has its greatest pull to inaction.

It really doesn't matter what you do. Make a pact with yourself that you will not stay in bed longer than a certain time and that you will go for a walk or grab a coffee or call a friend and arrange to meet up or even better go for a run. Start the motors again, get things moving and begin to create the mental and physical energy that you need to beat this trap.

The fourth trap of depression: Misperception and the inability to see or feel truth or reality

When someone is struggling in the mental funk and cloud of depression, one of the hardest things for them to access is any sense of objectivity about who they are, what is happening in their lives, and what it all "means".

The depressed person truly thinks and feels that their life is a mess and that something has absolutely and irrecoverably gone wrong. When they find that they are unable to do some of the simplest tasks or life routines like having a shower, preparing a meal, talking to a friend, or enjoying a walk outdoors, they may begin to fear that they will never be able to experience a normal life again. This is especially true for someone who has experienced severe and debilitating clinical depression.

Clinical depression is really just a term for someone whose symptoms on the scale of depression have become quite unbearable and have led to an almost complete loss of self and ability to operate normally or engage with life at all. It is obviously at these times that there is a major risk for suicidal ideation as the depressed person begins to lose hope that they will ever recover or feel normal again. This is a terrifying space to be in as a human being. I don't have to imagine what this is like because I have been there myself. Granted, everyone's experience of depression is unique but when it comes to some of the known symptoms, these things are very typical of the depressed state.

Someone who may be experiencing these thoughts and feelings for the first time may be quite shocked and surprised by the negativity of their own thinking. I often have clients who come to see me telling me how "this is not me" with a bewildered look on their face. I say, "You are right, this is not you...this is the depressed version of you and the way you are thinking right now cannot be relied on in any way at all as a true reflection of what is going on in your life."

They must understand that their own thinking process has become a trap. They have become a victim of an altered state of mind in which the ability to think clearly, objectively, positively and with any sort of perspective has been temporarily lost. If the person can at least somehow understand that part, it can help to release them from the trap. Awareness is always the first step to making any change in life. It is no different when it comes to this particularly heinous trap of depression. When we can somehow grasp – in the middle of a depressive experience – that our thoughts and emotions are *temporarily* untrustworthy – then we have a much greater chance of coming through it quicker.

When the depressed person buys into what their own mind is telling them, *that's* when the real trouble can begin.

There are some depressions which do not appear to come from anything situational, which is called atypical depression. It is chronic and generally does not seem to respond to any treatment at all. A good friend from South Africa lost his younger brother to this kind of depression. They tried everything to help him but nothing seemed to change his state and eventually he took his life which was just devastating to all of them. Even in his case, antidepressants were not the answer and may even have contributed to the mental hell that he went through towards the end.

Fortunately, this kind of intractable and unmovable depression is a very small percentage of the cases. I fully believe that most depressions are caused either by something that has gone wrong in the body or something that has "gone wrong" in someone's life situation. With regards to the body some of the causes could be, for example, hormonal issues, an underactive thyroid or even an overuse of antibiotic medications, which can be devastating to the gut's microbiome where most of our serotonin is produced. Anything that interferes with the body's ability to produce our most important neurotransmitters like dopamine, serotonin and noradrenalin has the potential to throw our mental and emotional systems out of whack and lead to anxiety and depression.

In these altered states of physiology and mental as well as emotional states of mind, one of the biggest traps is believing that any negative thoughts that we are having are actually real and true. We have to begin to understand on a very deep level that they just aren't and cannot be objective and even if there is some modicum of truth to them, we just need to know that if we are experiencing anxiety or depression that we are mostly being sold a lie by our own minds and we absolutely have to try with everything we have in us not to buy into any of that nonsense.

When we are being trapped by our own thoughts and emotions we have to realise that trying to THINK our way out of a THINKING trap is just ridiculous. We must accept that that particular avenue has been cut off, road-blocked and ambushed. We need to turn away from our own thinking and run away in the opposite direction from all the negativity. I said RUN away for a very specific reason, because when the avenue of relief from our thinking and feeling cannot be thinking itself, we need to change the mode of relief completely, and that is usually to make changes on the physical plane. This may include changing our diets and this is a critical component, but there is nothing—and I mean nothing—that has the power to break a deep negative thinking spiral like moderate aerobic-cardiovascular activity.

If you want to go straight into my discussion of this life-saving tool please head over to Chapter Six.

The fifth trap of depression: Believing in the diagnosis or label

We will talk much more about this in a later chapter but it is important to note here that once people are "diagnosed" with depression or an anxiety disorder, they start to define who they are and what kind of life is possible for them by that diagnosis. Luckily, I never bought into it. I KNEW at the core of my being that there was nothing wrong with me other than that I had been going through a really stressful time in my twenties just after finishing my degree, and then I was "diagnosed" as having GAD (general anxiety disorder) and told that I needed to be on antidepressants and that they would make me feel better than I had ever felt before in my life.

I now see this as a staggeringly inappropriate, irresponsible and unbelievably harmful statement to make to anyone, especially from any medical professional who has never really studied anxiety or depression in any depth, much less had their own lived experience of either of them and therefore knows what might work to heal them.

There is generally ZERO informed consent when it comes to explaining in detail all the pros and cons of taking an antidepressant. People are not warned at all about the side effects, not only in the short term but in the long term, and I certainly wasn't warned that I might possibly spend 17 years of my life trying to get off them, even when I felt that life was going well.

It is vitally important for anyone who was living a mostly normal life prior to being diagnosed with a label and being put onto antidepressants to completely refuse and disregard any such labels. It is a critical key to becoming free again and we will discuss this in much greater depth in Chapter Eleven.

The traps of anti-depressant drugs

Dr. Peter Breggin is one of the foremost experts on the subject of antidepressant drugs and their impact on the human brain. He is a passionate opponent of such drugs and the pharmaceutical complex that drives and peddles their sales to the unsuspecting public. Dr. Breggin is a psychiatrist himself who passionately believes in our human capability to heal without drugs, which alter just about everything about the human mind, body and spirit. Beyond opposing the over-prescription of antidepressants to an unsuspecting adult population, Dr. Breggin is a strong proponent of not drugging children, especially kids who have been "diagnosed" with ADHD (attention deficit hyperactive disorder).

Dr. Breggin coined the phrase "medication spellbinding" to refer to the altered state of consciousness that adults as well as teenagers and kids go through when their brains are being impacted by drugs which severely alter the way they think, feel and act. When it comes to class action lawsuits there is only one man the lawyers for the pharmaceutical companies fear, and that is Dr. Peter Breggin.

Coming back to the individual's experience of these drugs, most people are aware that there are side effects of going onto the drugs. These have been relatively widely publicized and were much more severe when it came to the older class of antidepressants, known as the "tricyclics". These heinous drugs were called "tri"-cyclic because they impacted three of the different and critical neurotransmitters in the human brain and body – dopamine, norepinephrine and serotonin. I won't go into the side effects of going onto these drugs as you can easily look this up online...if you want to have some nightmares for the next few weeks. However, what becomes trickier is understanding and coping with the side effects of remaining on these drugs over time and what begins to happen when someone tries to get off them. I am not only talking about the tricyclics but all the anti-anxiety and anti-depressant drugs.

You see, according to my understanding, the only thing that the pharmaceutical companies need to do in order to get a psychiatric drug approved to be sold to the general public is to run trials (called randomised controlled trials) for four to six weeks with a group of depressed patients either taking the experimental drug or being placed into a placebo group. If the researchers perceive the drug to have an effect greater than the placebo, then it is deemed safe and effective for public consumption, and the mass experimentation on humanity can continue unabated.

One of the most glaring problems with this approach is that there are very few, if any, longitudinal studies conducted by the very companies who release these drugs on the public to see what happens to these people who are placed on their drugs a few weeks later...a few months later...a few years later. I would place a wager that 90% of the people placed onto antidepressant drugs, if followed up only a few months or years later, would wish to God they had never been duped into taking them in the first place. I know this from the hundreds of people who have written to me over the five years since the first part of my story was published on the Mad in America website.

Randomised controlled trials do not have any record of what happened next. But the poor souls who kept taking the drugs in the hope that their quality of life would improve do. And in most cases, their lives have been severely negatively impacted and, in some cases, most tragically, their lives have been lost.

I will not go into detail about the ongoing and severe issues that people experience on these drugs but I will list some of the primary ones:

- Short term memory difficulties;
- Loss of libido and/or the full range of sensory sexual experience (which can and does clearly lead to intimate relationship difficulties and breakdowns);
- Weight gain;
- Facial and nervous tics and twitches;
- Heart problems;
- Liver disease;
- Difficulty accessing true emotions – love, joy, grief, sadness, excitement, peace;
- Amplification of anxious and depressive thoughts and emotions;
- Inability to be completely and fully present in the moment.

Given all of the above, it may be no wonder that people stuck on these drugs begin to act to get off them. But what happens when they try?

They begin to experience antidepressant drug withdrawal, euphemistically named "antidepressant discontinuation syndrome" by the drug companies — another way of isolating and ostracising as well as shaming the poor souls caught in the trap.

In a recent study conducted in New Zealand, only 1% of the 1829 (Read et al., 2014)[2] people who were surveyed who were taking anti-depressants said that they had been warned about any chance of experiencing withdrawal symptoms should they try to come off the medications; 27% of the respondents reported that they were "addicted" to the drugs and couldn't get off them.

I too had a very long and agonising journey with being prescribed anti-depressants (citalopram) back in March 2000, when I had just turned twenty-four years old. I had just had another panic attack after receiving my master's thesis back from my supervisor with red pen all over it and so my mother took me to see a psychiatrist. The psychiatrist discussed my life history and "diagnosed" me with GAD (general anxiety disorder) and wrote a script for me to take citalopram – one of the newest anti-depressant SSRI's at the time which was said to be even better than Prozac due to it having less side effects. I wasn't sure what to do.

The psychiatrist never mentioned a word about the potential hell that you can experience in the first four to six weeks of taking an anti-depressant. She never spoke about any remote possibility that there might be an issue if I one day tried to come off them. I was just told, you have this "diagnosis" and this medication will help you feel better than you have felt in your life.

I began taking the medication and within a week, I not only felt that my anxiety skyrocketed out of control but I also fell into a deep, dark hole. I was immobilised in my own mind. And knowing what I know now, I can see that the drugs actually fueled my depression and anxiety even further before I began to feel somewhat normal and able to function about two months later.

---

[2] https://www.sciencedirect.com/science/article/pii/S01651781140008 3

I knew I didn't want to be on them long term and so I managed to wean myself off about a year later but started taking them again in May 2004 after undergoing one of the worst medical interventions I have experienced in my life, called an osteotomy. That story will have to be for another time but suffice to say it involved a surgeon slicing through my skull and moving my top jaw forward which led to a terrible and debilitating recovery as well as ongoing nerve damage which I still suffer from to this day.

It was then, in May of 2004, because of the severe impact that the operation had on me and my need to get back on my feet and back to my then wife in London, that I started taking an antidepressant again. This time it was Paxil (Paroxetine), and while I was eventually able to get on with my life, I had no idea that I had just began a journey for the battle of my life.

It is quite odd thinking back now, that I started taking antidepressants for the second time at exactly the same time, May of 2004, that I was told that my former master in Tae Kwon Do (who had been a mentor in my life from the ages of eighteen to twenty-four) had passed away from stomach cancer. He had been a very influential part of my late teens and early twenties and had been my mentor for almost seven years so hearing of his passing really affected me at the time.

During the next fourteen years of my life, from the ages of twenty-seven to forty-one, I got married, left my friends, family and entire life in South Africa; went to live in London for eighteen months where I struggled with major anxiety and depression; immigrated to Sydney Australia; struggled with major anxiety and depression again; experienced becoming a father to two amazing little boys; got divorced; went through a complete turnaround in my career by moving out of the field of human resources and back into psychology as a counsellor and trainer; and then went through the unbelievably painful experience of meeting a woman who told me she couldn't become pregnant and then did, which is the reason that

I have my beautiful little girl Lily, who is now five years old. We lived together for about eighteen months and then split up when Lily was just four months old. I then spent the next five years being a single father to three children, whilst counselling approximately thirty people a week.

This is a very difficult thing to go through when you are not taking anti-depressants and it is infinitely HARDER when you are taking them. The reason is that the anti-depressant and anti-anxiety medications will actually be aggravating if not actually causing some of the anxiety and depression that you are experiencing.

Sometimes, when people have moved through painful experiences such as the ones I did but have come out the other side, they begin to realise that things aren't adding up. They realise that there is no obvious reason for them to feel THAT anxious or depressed when things seem to have calmed down. People also experience unbelievable anxiety and/or depression when they try to reduce or taper off these medications, and at first, they mostly look to their own circumstances for the cause of their discomfort or anguish. If there is no obvious trigger in their circumstances or environment, they will be told that it is "their anxiety" or "their depression" coming back.

Most people don't think to question this. Why on earth would I feel anxiety or depression just because I have stopped taking a medication? Surely, once things have settled down in my life and I feel ready to come off the medications (which I never needed before in my life before I started to take them), I should be able to come off them.

It is understandable that one should come off them slowly. However, if I do it very slowly and after I have taken the last bit of tablet, and I suddenly experience massive anxiety or depression again, how could that possibly be my depression returning? Does that mean that the anti-depressants only masked or covered up my depression, keeping me emotionally numb and unable to really function as I wanted to in life?

If I suddenly stop taking them, is it just logical and expected that I should get knocked right over by my suppressed anxiety and/or depression? Was it really just lurking there all along and the drugs just suppress my anxiety and depression only as long as I stay on them? But, why do I crash so fast and with seemingly little changed in my actual life when I try to come off them? This is a very important question that anyone who experiences a major reaction such as this when trying to stop antidepressants must keep in mind and look for answers to. It is certainly what I did but I had no way of knowing what the truth was or whether I would indeed ever be able to get off them and be okay.

Surely it is better to WORK THROUGH our thoughts and feelings that are producing the anxiety and depression in the first place and then return to living our lives rather than live a "half-life" still shrouded in anxiety and depression anyway being ON the medication.

As I have mentioned before, I got stuck in this terrible nightmare for 17 years. There were many ups and downs of life happening during that time frame of course, but with hindsight, I know for sure that the drugs hampered my ability to recover quicker and for the long term. This became especially true when I tried to taper off the drugs, time and time again. If I had to try to describe the depths of my struggles mentally, emotionally and physically here it would take up a whole book in itself…maybe one day it will be. However, I can try to provide a brief insight at least into some of the things I tried during those 17 years to get off antidepressants and overcome anxiety and depression. During all of this time I was usually engaged in some form of counselling and I continued to work on my thoughts and beliefs using cognitive behaviour therapy. My appetite to discover – usually through books – the answers to overcoming anxiety and depression as well as the antidepressants became an obsession.

During that time, I tried just about anything and everything you can imagine to get off them, including:

- Tapering slowly with a system of monitoring every symptom during withdrawal and trying to tell the difference between a withdrawal reaction and a real emotion or physical problem I may have been experiencing. I did this with daily recorded journals of everything including what I ate, drank, how I slept, whether I exercised or not, and what my thoughts and moods were. I did this in the hope of identifying what was a withdrawal reaction and what was not.
- Switching to longer acting anti-depressants such as Prozac to assist with a more gradual taper which didn't produce such a shock to the system (which is something every doctor should know and usually they don't). I only found out this massive key to my eventual success by accident when the psychiatrist I was seeing happened to mention that Prozac had the longest half-life of all the antidepressants.
- Going onto a very disciplined regimen of supplements aimed at boosting brain functioning and serotonin levels "naturally" which included ingesting large amounts of fish oils, vitamin B, C and D as well as various herbs to support the adrenal system.
- Regular exercising – albeit not every day and certainly not with the consistency and vigor that I do now – not even close. However, at one stage I was running about three times a week for about five kilometers. This certainly helped me but was never the solution to helping me com-

pletely overcome the anxiety, depression or the anti-depressants.

- Meditating – I began to practice meditation on a more regular basis and found it to be very helpful in alleviating stress, negative thinking and assisting in elevating one's mood and energy levels. However, once again, just exercising a few times a week, taking all the "right" supplements and meditating never got me off the anti-depressant medications. There was one exception in 2013, the year my daughter Lily was born; I managed to get off them completely for a period of six months after doing very regular exercise and using Prozac to taper off them. However, I ended up having to take them again in January 2014. I do, however, think that meditation i.e. learning to calm the mind, body and emotions is critical to success and so I have devoted a whole chapter to this.
- I also researched and tried something called "The road back programme" by Jim Harper who is a bio-pharmacist who has dedicated much of his professional life to researching how to help people get off medications using natural supplements (which he created) that weren't commercially available. These included mixtures meant to restore deficiencies created in the body and brain from extensive use of anti-depressant and anti-anxiety medications. I tried these for over a year and aside from finding the neuro-calm product to be somewhat helpful in alleviating anxiety, it didn't achieve the results I was hoping for.

My journey and research then continued into looking at food and the connection between what we eat and mood, stress, anxiety, depression and general mental health. I found much research on this topic and discovered things like the impact of the bio-dome in the gut and how the production of serotonin could be hampered or lowered due to various issues related to the gut. However, in and of itself this never helped me get off the anti-depressants completely and whenever I was on a low dose and something very stressful happened in my life, I would be knocked back down and end up having to push the dose back up again.

My concerns about the impact of long-term use of anti-depressants continued to grow. I experienced some incredibly difficult and harrowing experiences with the medication as well as some very concerning side effects which began to appear over time – including lashing out at night in my sleep, struggling to identify my true emotions about things, ringing in my ears, short-term memory loss and desensitisation of my senses. Another concern was the impact that taking the medications was having on my organs and in particular my liver. Blood tests began to identify elevated liver counts which the doctors said could only come from excessive alcohol consumption or potentially the medications. I never drank much alcohol in my life, so I knew what was causing the elevated liver count issue.

I remained absolutely determined to come off the anti-depressants. But it seemed every time I tried it ended with me getting into a deeper hole than I had ever been before. At one point, I was very close to going into a hospital bed. But I persisted and pushed through each time and got my life back on track. But it was never really on track; at least I didn't feel it was. I knew that I was so much more and had so much more potential than the "facts" and "realities" of my life seemed to be indicating.

Every time I tried to get off them, no matter how slowly, I crashed and burned and medical "experts" as well as the people closest to me would say I was being ridiculous trying to get off them. They may not have always said it directly to me but essentially, they were telling me that I should just accept my fate and keep taking these drugs that I KNEW were ruining my health and my life. I also knew that I was running out of time because the side effects and ever-increasing long-term effects were becoming more and more obvious to me. My health was beginning to suffer and when I received blood tests back showing an elevated liver count, I knew that if I didn't do something soon it would be too late. I had also come across quite a few people who were now suffering with tics (facial and body movements which they couldn't control), heart disease that had sprung up with no family history or risk, and a huge range of other debilitating physical conditions.

Very few, if any, of those closest to you and certainly not your doctor, psychiatrist or even your (sorry to say) counsellor or psychologist will truly believe that a big part of what you are struggling with is very much directly connected to the antidepressant drugs, especially if you are attempting to taper off or withdraw from them.

It was, however, from late 2017 that I really took massive action and began to implement everything that you will read about in the rest of this book, which led to me successfully overcoming anxiety, depression and finally – after 17 very painful and treacherous years – getting off the antidepressants for good.
I have thus learned some very important traps that you need to be aware of when it comes to the antidepressants and what you can do to avoid getting caught in them.

The first trap of antidepressants: Physiological withdrawal and emotional havoc

Of course, the first and most obvious trap would be the physical and potentially devastating emotional impact on someone who stops taking a drug which has been altering his or her body and brain chemistry artificially for any period of time. The brain and body take four to six weeks to adjust going *onto* these drugs when someone first starts taking them (and let me tell you what hell that process is). So, the idea that you can just stop taking the drugs cold turkey is beyond ridiculous to me but seems a very commonplace practice when the patient visits their doctor complaining about the drug and wanting to stop taking it. Having said this, more doctors are becoming aware that their patients cannot just stop taking these drugs

But, why do so many doctors still think that a mind-altering drug can just be stopped but would never dream of telling someone to just go cold turkey with any other major illicit drug? Would you "just stop" taking cocaine? Can you "just stop" smoking? Maybe some people can but most people can't. Why is that? Because they go into a withdrawal from something as relatively benign as nicotine. Nicotine! In fact, if you were to go to Dr. Breggin's website and watch one of his very first videos you will see him give a very simple example from his own life where he found himself feeling a bit down and agitated for a few days and was very concerned about why he was feeling that way until his wife yelled out one morning from the kitchen that she had mistakenly placed decaffeinated coffee in the coffee jar! And, as he rightly says, if caffeine can have that kind of an impact on his thoughts and mood through withdrawal, just imagine what a drug like an antidepressant can do that alters neuro-chemicals in your brain!

You see, the pharmaceutical companies would never in a million years have been able to sell these drugs so easily if they had had to warn doctors and the public that there might be a severe withdrawal problem for their patients when they tried to come off them once their life crisis had passed and they were ready to live their lives again.

When someone reduces the drug too quickly or goes "cold turkey", their body and mind go into a drug withdrawal reaction and they begin to experience physical as well as mental and emotional withdrawal reactions, including: electric "zap"-like sensations, vertigo, tinnitus, muscle spasms, increased agitation, anxiety and depression, which is to be expected if you suddenly and dramatically reduce the amount of serotonin, dopamine and norepinephrine in the body and brain.

But when the patient returns to the doctor with these symptoms, they are mistaken for a "return" of their anxiety or depression which they may have last struggled with many years ago. Invariably, the doctor or psychiatrist will insist that the patient needs to go back onto the drug, increase what they are taking or try another drug altogether. And the human experimentation continues.

The second trap of antidepressants – The trauma returns

The subconscious mind is quite amazing. We know that when we dream, things that we have been contemplating, struggling with, ignoring and pushing away seem to rise to the surface of our consciousness in the form of dreams.

This is why some of the most influential psychologists who have walked this planet were so fascinated by dreams, including Sigmund Freud and Carl Jung. As human beings, we seem to persist in the error of thinking that if we mask something, maybe push it away, take a pill for it, drink some alcohol or any other manner of obliterating our conscious awareness of the pain, grief, or fear that it will somehow, magically go away. But it NEVER goes away...not on its own. Not without our attention to it. Not without our PROCESSING of it and coming to terms with it. And the antidepressant drugs do no more than a Band-Aid would do to a gunshot wound or poisonous snake bite when it comes to true healing and recovery from some of the traumatic events and experiences that we go through in this life.

So, as the person starts to taper off the drugs and their brain begins to wake up and their subconscious is finally allowed to have a voice again, all hell breaks loose. And it is no wonder, is it? The original fear, trauma, grief, sadness, or life event rises back to the surface, asking to be processed and worked through. Unfortunately for many, the pain of those returning feelings, thoughts and memories becomes a little unbearable and they just want relief from it because they may not be ready to face it or they don't have the right support in place or they have not done enough preparation physically, mentally, emotionally and spiritually to handle the kick-back from tapering off the drugs. This is why it is imperative that anyone who is thinking of reducing their antidepressants is at least able to say they have tried to work through some of their issues, even while on the drugs, because it is infinitely better to have done some of that work before than to try come off and be totally unprepared for all the pain and trauma to return.

If done with foresight and with enough preparation and work, the landing will be much smoother and will provide a much greater chance of the person coming off the drug successfully.

This is something which I personally struggled through when coming off antidepressants as did most of those who I know who came off them. There are things that have caused us pain in life. I don't know what it is for you but I am willing to bet it has something to do with the people you love or loved in the past, or your sense of meaning and purpose in life, or the pain of having to suffer through times of financial stress and difficulty or the trauma of having been abused or hurt in some way. The drugs have helped us cope and get on with our lives, because that's what we needed to do. But, we have paid a price for that coping and at some point there are those of us who realise that staying on the drugs is no longer an option either because we are now experiencing worse effects from being on them for so long which are now becoming dangerous to our very lives or because we have realised that we are not truly connecting mentally, emotionally and even spiritually to the world around us the way we were meant to.

I had my work to do too. As a divorced father of three children, I struggled terribly with being apart from my gorgeous kids. I would get triggered constantly on weekends when I was not with them and saw other fathers with their kids – even though I see my kids every single Tuesday night and half of every single weekend, the trauma and sorrow of not being with them as much as I want to and feeling like I am missing out on part of them growing up can really take me down an emotional spiral and feels like my heart is being torn apart.

Even now, as a I write this, there are some tears welling up. But, what I have learned to do, especially now that I know these thoughts and feelings cannot hurt me and that there are no noxious chemicals making me feel like this, is to process and sit with those feelings of sadness and grief and know that I will be alright. I have also had to learn to practice reframing my situation…which is to say that I look for another way to look at my life and realise that my bond and my connection to my children does not change just because we don't spend as much time together as a traditional family. And, there are some families where the father is hardly there anyway, even though he technically "lives" with them.

The reason I share this very intimate and quite vulnerable part of my life story is to provide a very real example of just how difficult this particular trap of coming off antidepressants can be. If I had not done the work beforehand, I may have panicked at the first sign of trouble and gone back onto them. But, I have way too much knowledge and experience for that now. I have come to understand that we are meant to feel our emotions, and that most of all we should not be afraid of them. Emotions are like waves, they come and go. They can be mild and harmless or they can be wild, raging and crash us against the rocks. But, we will not die if we can learn to float and ride those waves because eventually the sea settles, the clouds DO clear and we see things in a different light – sometimes literally – and our feelings lift.

And so, it is my strongest encouragement to you if you are currently struggling to do the work of talking, writing, reading, running, meditating, breathing, crying, singing, and even laughing to help you work through those painful thoughts and feelings that will arise as you begin to taper off the drugs. Let me also say here that you may decide to remain on the drugs and that is completely your choice and personal freedom to do so and there is absolutely no judgement here from me.

It was my choice and my decision to get off the drugs at any cost because I knew that they were creating a barrier between me and my complete healing and full recovery but I did a lot of work prior to succeeding and as you have seen, I tried once before in 2013 and ended up back on them. I was over the moon and so happy to be off them and thought that I was finally done with them and then, after only six months, fell over and ended up back on them for the next four years. So, I guess you could say I'm a bit of a veteran when it comes to the process of tapering. I am now delighted every single day to wake up without anxiety coursing through my body and mind and I have come to realise that, for me, my most horrible day off the antidepressants is still better than any average day I had on them.

The third trap of antidepressants: Dosage dilemmas and horror stories

Trying to decide how much you can safely reduce a dose without having a major withdrawal reaction is a major trap and difficulty people experience as they start to investigate how to get off antidepressants. On the one hand it is important to understand what is happening to you when you are going into withdrawal, as it helps to prepare you and takes away a bit of the fear concerning some of the physical, mental and emotional symptoms that you are likely to experience. However, there is another problem with getting too much into every little detail and monitoring your every symptom. The problem is that you may become hyper-focused on every little thing that is happening in your mind and body and then freak out every time you experience something "out of the ordinary".

In addition, there are those who are quite happy to share their horror stories online in support forums and who freely share their negativity and hopelessness about getting off antidepressants or benzodiazepines. Getting caught up in that kind of negativity is never going to help anyone wean off antidepressants. That is because they are setting up a belief system that it is extremely hard, if not impossible, to get off the drugs. However, that may not be the case *for them*, especially if they have done everything they can to prepare themselves for the tapering and have done the work: physically, mentally, emotionally and spiritually. I say spiritually not in any religious sense (even though I am sure many people who have gotten off have relied on their faith to help them) but more in the sense of connecting to something beyond themselves. It is an expansion of thinking to higher levels of awareness and consciousness, which can often be gained through practices such as meditation. I practiced meditation very regularly as part of my preparation before coming off the antidepressants and it always led to feelings of calm and peace that were incredibly uplifting and provided me with much hope that I had the capacity to settle my anxiety down. There are also many natural foods and supplements which can assist with anxiety and depression which I will discuss in chapter five.

There are so many opinions about how to get off antidepressants and some of them include suggestions that you have to microdose by dropping the medication by approximately 10% every three to four weeks. I don't know if you have ever tried to reduce a 10mg tablet by 10% before but let me tell you it's not much fun and similar to trying to split the atom with a paring knife. Not that I would know how hard it is to split an atom but I think for us lay people, it's probably right up there in its difficulty level!

This leads to people getting unbelievably frustrated and to further anxiety and fear about how best to reduce their drug dosage without falling back into unbearable anxiety and depression. However, depending on which drug you are trying to come off, you could very well end up in withdrawal regardless of how slow or how small you taper the drug, and you never know when it will hit you and most unsettling, you may never know exactly why it had that effect on you or what you "did wrong".

And so, getting caught up in everyone else's experience of coming off antidepressants and their horror stories is never going to help someone get off antidepressants successfully.

Each person should be doing as much objective research as they can, learning from the real experts in this field like Dr. Peter Breggin, Robert Whitaker, Dr. Joseph Glenmullen, Prof. Peter C. Gøtzsche and Dr. Elliot Valenstein.

Beyond this, each individual needs to test everything out for themselves to see if it applies to them and what their physical, mental and emotional reactions are to any particular strategy or step they take, and then adjust accordingly. What works for me will not necessarily work for you; however, you may want to at least give some of the safer strategies a test, which is what the remainder of this book will focus on.

The fourth trap of antidepressants: Becoming psychologically reliant

One of the hardest things that someone who is going to succeed at getting off antidepressants or anti-anxiety tablets is going to have to do is move beyond the trap of becoming psychologically attached or reliant on the drug being the one and only thing that makes him or her feel better. What I am referring to is that not only is there clearly a physical dependence on the drug due to the obvious withdrawal effects when we try to stop them but there is also the psychological dependence where we feel safe knowing that the drugs are there to "save" us and help us cope and feel better and get on with our lives. Learning to undo this knot and learning how to let go of the dependence psychologically is key and it begins with realising that you have infinite resources both within you and from the world around you that can help shift your mental and emotional state from anxiety and depression back to peace, calm and happiness. And most important of all that you can find these options and you can learn how to use them and set yourself free of the need to depend on a drug for your mental and emotional wellbeing.

These are some of the traps when it comes to trying to get off antidepressants and one of the absolutely critical keys to doing it successfully is stepping away from everything you think you know about the subject and forgetting it all. This is because you can become caught up in one particular dogma and then miss out on some of the simplest and most effective things that you can do to prepare yourself to come off slowly and successfully.

Among the things that I had to work hard on shifting before I was able to finally let go of anxiety, depression and the antidepressants were the underlying **beliefs** that had been created in me that I was somehow unable to function in life without them or that I was just someone who had to suffer and struggle with anxiety and depression, probably for the rest of my life.

This is what the next chapter is all about and it is absolutely critical that you reflect on your beliefs about anxiety, depression and antidepressants which includes whether you want to buy into the idea that some people just have to be on these drugs forever.

CHAPTER TWO

Changing your beliefs

"Our greatest dreams are never out of reach, only out of belief"

Dr. Wayne Dyer

Beliefs are probably your most powerful ally in overcoming anxiety and depression in your life. They are also your worst enemy and have the greatest power to keep you stuck in anxiety and depression indefinitely. Why is that?

It is because you can only act on the beliefs that you have in your mind. In psychology we learn about the conscious and subconscious minds. We are taught that the subconscious is very powerful and can rule our behaviour. Beliefs are like electricity, because in and of themselves they are a neutral force, but depending on how they are used, they have the power to take you down into misery and pain or they have the power to lift you up and sometimes, they can save your life. You get to choose, even though you may have a *belief* that you don't actually get to make those kinds of choices.

You may say things to yourself such as "this is just the way it is", "this is how I have always been", "it's my personality", "it's my nature", "it's in my family", or "it's all I've ever known".

These are all beliefs and they are also, my friend, complete and utter lies that you are choosing to continue to believe. Yes, I said you are CHOOSING to continue to believe these lies. It is time to re-examine everything you have ever told yourself, or anyone else has ever told you, about who you really are, what you are capable of, what you can achieve and who you will be in this life. You have free will; you get to choose. Unless you are in jail, you have most of the human freedoms to think, act and be whoever you want to be. And guess what? Even if you ARE in jail, you still get to choose who you want to be, like a certain jailbird named Nelson Mandela, who was locked away in jail for 27 years in South Africa. Just think briefly about the options Nelson Mandela had when he was sentenced to life in prison. Facing potentially the rest of his life on an isolated island off the coast of Cape Town, doing hard manual labour in the sun every day, what choices do you think Mandela had? The freedoms that most of us take for granted, such as where he wanted to go, who he wanted to talk to, when he wanted to go to the toilet, what he wanted to eat or drink, were all taken away from him.

However, just as another prisoner named Victor Frankl discovered in the Nazi concentration camps in Auschwitz during the Second World War, when he faced imminent torture and death on a daily basis, you still have the ultimate human freedom: the freedom of your will and your desire to live. I very specifically did not say the freedom of your own mind because I know what happens when we get depressed. I have described it as becoming a prisoner in your own mind. Locked in, shut down, with what you believe to be "no chance of parole".

However, even though the avenue of pure freedom of thought may not be open to you because your mind is shrouded by the dark cloud of depression, your will to live and your decision to *never give up*, no matter how you feel and no matter what life seems to be throwing at you, is the *one thing* that will ensure that you will come through it. Because nothing - and I mean *nothing* - can beat the human spirit which still has the desire to live.

So, determine right now that you will not be the one to decide whether things are over for you or not. Let the universe decide. You just get on with living and don't look back.

You may have to, as Dr. Wayne Dyer says during his speeches, "give up your personal history" and more importantly you must "re-write your agreement with reality".

What did he mean by this? Well, he meant although you have come to this world as a tabula rasa (blank slate), that didn't last very long. From the day you were born you began to perceive and make sense of the world around you. As you grew, you perceived your mother or father or both. And whilst you began to explore this world on your own, you were being guided by the beliefs, hopes, fears, insecurities, opinions, and behaviours of those closest to you.

In most cases, if you didn't conform with what those carers wanted or expected from you - especially as you got older and began to assert your freedom and independence of thought and will - you may have had a sense that if you went up against them, you might land up on the streets. You had no means of supporting yourself as a child and even as a teenager and in some rare cases, even as an adult.

So, what did this mean for your thinking, your beliefs and your behaviours? You had to follow the rules. You had to conform, or at least act as if you were.

Some seem to be able to buck this very formative, powerful and influential impact on their thoughts and beliefs in life. Most don't dare to contemplate that they would even have an option to think in a different, more independent and self-reliant manner.

However, as we move into the teen, young adult and more mature years we begin to see that what our parents/carers believed and how they behaved while we were small and malleable is not necessarily what we now believe or how we now choose to perceive the world and universe around us. It is then that we may begin to make new and deliberate choices in our lives, unencumbered by the beliefs, thoughts, biases and conditions of our parents or others who shaped our thinking and beliefs growing up.

This is in the ideal world. And of course, the primary influencers on our thinking shift as we get older. It begins with those most primary carers in our lives and then it can shift, depending on who we come into contact with during the course of our lives.

The most influential people on our thinking, beliefs and behaviours can then shift to siblings, aunts, uncles, grandparents, religious figures, friends, peers, mentors, coaches etc.

However, all along this pathway, many people never stop to think about just exactly who these people are who are influencing their thinking, their beliefs as well as their emotions and behaviours. Most people do not stop to evaluate if they have been influenced, taken advice from, and are now living their lives from the perspective of someone who is actually worthy of being imitated or followed. There is nothing more telling about whether one should or should not follow the advice of anyone around you than the results those people are showing in their own lives. One should ALWAYS strive to understand the thinking, beliefs and motivations of those who try to influence us to a way of thinking, being or doing.

Those who do not critically evaluate where the advice they follow so religiously actually comes from are doomed to live a life that is not their own and which may lead them down pathways they never intended to tread.

This is not to say there is no turning back or no second or even third chances in this life. I believe it is never too late to make a new distinction, to discover a new truth about your life or life in general and thus begin immediately to make new choices and move your life in a completely different direction.

Breaking free of my own negative beliefs

I thought I would share with you some of the truths and realities of my life that I absolutely believed to be real which I have completely turned on their heads and dissolved:

I used to believe that I was not an early riser and that I could never get up early and exercise like all those other freaks I would see running around before the birds even woke up **until** .... one day in January 2018, after being prodded by my Tae Kwon Do master to go for a run at 4am because I couldn't sleep, it all turned around. After having not done much running at all over the prior two or so years, because I had built another negative and false belief that strenuous exercise actually could make my anxiety and depression worse, I started running at around 5:00 am every single morning. I started with running three kilometers. When I first began running again, I was SERIOUSLY unfit. I had to stop multiple times during my run to catch my breath and then carry on.

As weeks rolled by, I increased the running to 4kms and then 5kms and then I started running longer distances at least once every weekend until I got up to 8kms and then 10 and then 12kms. These runs are done at around 5am, every single day, when it's dark, when it's cold as hell sometimes, when it's lightly drizzling rain, when I have my kids with me and when I don't, when I am in Sydney or when I am not, when it's a public holiday and when it's not. It doesn't matter that it's 05h00 – as Robin Williams said in Good Morning Vietnam: "What does the O stand for? Oh my God, it's early!"

Aside from playing a big part in helping me elevate my energy levels and finally break free from the antidepressant drugs, the running in that early morning time provides a sacred time and space for me to clear my mind and meditatively run along, contemplating my life and what is happening in it. In fact, most of the chapters and major ideas for this book came out of my early morning runs.

So, I have gone from being someone who believes he is not a morning person when it comes to getting up early and exercising to being someone that even high level athletes are admiring. All it took was challenging the belief and deciding it was just nonsense and a petty excuse that was just keeping me from experiencing something truly remarkable in life. Going the extra mile…literally!

I used to believe that I needed six to eight hours of sleep in order to function and be happy and well…until I started getting only about three to four hours of unbroken sleep a night. This came on the back of the increase to my cardiovascular activity, mostly through my running each morning, as well as the changes to my diet and finally being able to get off the antidepressant drugs completely. I now know, that we only really need around four to six hours of sleep to function. We may not be functioning at our highest levels – just ask any parent with a newborn – but we can actually handle life with less hours of sleep than is traditionally sprouted if we are doing other things like eating well, exercising, meditating as well as limiting alcohol and any other negative substances.

I used to believe that I had to eat breakfast every morning because breakfast was "the most important meal of the day". This is something the breakfast cereal companies completely fabricated in order to sell you more puffed rice and sugar snacks that they actually call a nutritious meal! Then I started – once again at the insistence of my Tae Kwon Do master – to skip breakfast and do what is known as a caloric restriction diet. This requires that after dinner, you give your stomach and all your organs – especially the liver and kidneys – a chance to rest and repair. We are constantly bombarding our bodies with material to process, whether it's drinks, snacks or food. However, the body then doesn't have the time to cleanse itself or repair any damage done before we bombard it with more to process. Is it any wonder our bodies eventually start to break down and turn on us? Beyond the repairing part, when the body needs to process food – especially heavy foodstuffs such as animal protein – it has to work hard and this requires energy that we may need for other functions and activities that are so important for our mental health, wellbeing and productivity in life.

As I began to skip breakfast and basically just have a coffee during the morning and possibly a piece of gluten-free toast or a piece of fruit around mid-morning, I started to notice that it actually wasn't hard at all and that I just looked forward to lunch and dinner more. And as the days went by, rather than experiencing what everyone kept telling me I would – a lack of energy and possibly some other fate even more dire – I started to notice the complete opposite effect. My energy levels began to rise and rise. I started to feel lighter, calmer, clearer, cleaner and more focused. While everyone around me was chowing down on their greasy McMuffins and toasted cheese and hams, I would be sipping my flat white with almond and just observing the obsession we have with food. I would even go so far as to say the *addiction* we seem to have with food. More on that subject coming up in Chapter Five.

I used to believe that you needed protein (animal protein mostly, such as meat, chicken, eggs, milk) in order to have a "well-balanced" diet but when I changed my diet to predominantly rice, vegetables (especially my go-to dinner, which is cabbage, onion, garlic, celery and carrot soup with gluten-free bread), and other gluten-free products, with little to no sugar, I discovered that I felt lighter, calmer, more energetic, more focused, happier and healthier. Even my skin cleared after a few weeks! I struggled with red and dry skin around my nose and forehead for years and suddenly POOF, my skin started looking so much better. It's not perfect, especially in winter, but the red scaly skin has disappeared completely. Magic? Today, I get most of my protein from fish and eggs. I am not insane enough to think we can survive without *some* protein, but we certainly don't need the amounts of protein that nearly everyone thinks we do – especially from animals.

I used to believe that I needed certain vitamins, minerals and other supplements - which we apparently can't get enough of from our diets - in order to enjoy optimum mental and physical health. WRONG. I turned this belief right on its head. As I began to run every morning, eat vegetable soup, rice and then added smoked salmon and other fish or vegetarian-based protein meals, I noticed that I began to feel so much better physically and mentally. At the time, around December 2017, I had been taking fish oils and a range of other supplements every single morning. I used to take a little zip lock plastic bag with me every day and then have to take the supplements at varying times of the day – some with food because they could upset the stomach on their own. When I started to talk with my Tae Kwon Do master again, after being led to believe he had been dead for so long, and I told him what I was trying to do and all the supplements I was taking, he basically said to me and I quote, "EVERYTHING OUT!" and that's what I did. I immediately stopped everything and, along with the other dietary changes and increased exercise, began to feel more energetic, more focused, and more joyful than I had in decades. I have, however, reintroduced some supplements such as Vitamin D during the winter months as we really don't get enough of it without the sunshine and there are others from time to time such as Vitamin C that I may take. However, on the whole, my body is functioning extremely well without a whole bag of vitamins and supplements.

I used to believe that I might have a "chemical imbalance" in my brain which was causing a lack of serotonin and that was why I would get so anxious or depressed until I read Robert Whitaker's best-selling book *Anatomy of an Epidemic* and it completely turned my life around. I will never forget that fateful day when I was in a training session with some colleagues on how to deliver mental health awareness workshops to employees and managers and somehow the discussion of psychiatric medications came up.

I mentioned the fact that the training seemed to ignore the issue of the impact of antidepressants on an employee's mental wellbeing and that managers, supervisors and team leaders often know little to nothing about the impacts these drugs could be having on their employees' mental health, productivity, behaviour, performance and attendance at work.

However, this particular not-for-profit organisation – which has a very large presence in Australia – was very clear that we were not to talk about the antidepressant medications in any way. I didn't understand how we could completely ignore something that was a key driver in the reason so many people aren't getting better over time.

At that time, back in 2012, I really wasn't sure whether the theory about serotonin being the culprit was true or not or whether some people just had a need for these drugs because of some faulty wiring in the brain that suddenly seemed to lead to a lowered level of serotonin. However, regardless of this, a female colleague asked me if I had read the book *Anatomy of an Epidemic* by Robert Whitaker, which she said detailed the history of psychiatric drugs. She said I would find it to be an "interesting read". Little did I know that her off-the-cuff suggestion would lead to a complete revolution in my life and set me on the path to where I am today…drug free at last and feeling like I have been given a second chance at life and ever so grateful to my colleague for suggesting Robert's amazing book. When the book arrived, I was hooked from the first page and devoured the whole book. As each revelation jumped out at me from the page, my anger and my sense of vindication grew and grew.

What I had been trying to hold onto for dear life for almost 12 years at that stage was the hope that what a part of my consciousness had kept telling me was in fact true. It kept telling me gently that I DIDN'T have a chemical imbalance or something genetically wrong with the way my brain and body created serotonin, or any other neurotransmitter, for that matter! And as I got farther and farther into my reading of Robert's book, a conviction began to grow in me that it was time to throw that belief right out the window. I remember meeting up with my mother in the city one morning, which was a rare event as she was hardly ever in the city, and reading some of the book to her. I could see the skepticism in her eyes.

You see, she had been through hell with me over the years and she had seen the worst of it with me and she was nothing but terrified that I was going to attempt to get off the antidepressant drugs and fail hopelessly yet again. However, as I read some of the stories in Robert's book, especially about some of the young men and women who had taken their own lives or died due to the impact the drugs had on them, I noticed something in her eyes for the first time that day: a tiny spark of doubt about what she and I and most of the world have been brainwashed into believing, which is that anxiety and depression are caused by a lack of serotonin and that antidepressant drugs are the most effective and safe way to heal and save people. But Robert's book so clearly uncovered and blew out of the water everything the psychiatric community (or let's say most of the practitioners in it) and especially the pharmaceutical companies want us all to believe.

And so, armed with the knowledge and the absolute hope that I could finally overcome the drugs and be free, I found out that Prozac was the drug with the longest half-life (i.e. it remains in your system the longest and exits slower than the other drugs) and I switched across from what I had been taking at the time and began to taper. At the same time, I increased my cardiovascular activity, which I had been doing already with my then-partner and mother of my daughter. It was around July of 2013, only two months after my daughter was born (thirteen years after first being prescribed an antidepressant for anxiety) and only one month before my "relationship" with Lily's mother came to an abrupt and traumatic end, that I was able to get off the antidepressants completely and with little to no major withdrawal effects. However, that wonderful experience and freedom was short-lived and six months later, in January of 2014, after suffering the breakup with my little angel's mother and then changing careers and feeling like I had made an existentially horrifying mistake, I crashed and found myself having to start taking an antidepressant yet again. The story of what happened from January 2014 up until January 2018 is enough material for another entire book on its own.

However, by February 2018 I was finally free of the antidepressant drugs and this time, with the knowledge, experience and understanding that I gained over the previous four years, I was ready to remain off them forever.

With the other faulty beliefs I had concerning exercise, sleep and diet being challenged and destroyed, I was able to get off the drugs at a speed that should not have even been possible!

I also attribute part of my success in coming off the antidepressants to turning my attention almost completely away from the drugs and focusing only on what I was doing with my eating, my exercising, my meditating and my renewed energy and focus. And as I did, I began to lower the dose and tested how my mind and body reacted. I didn't breathe a word of it to those who I knew would push against me doing it. As Dr. Wayne Dyer would say, you have to keep these ideas about what you wish to achieve in your life very safe and in a sanctuary in your own mind. As soon as you speak to others about what it is you want to achieve or strive for you will invoke their ego and then the battle is half lost already. People might have a belief or image of you in their minds or worse, YOU might and probably do have an image and concept of yourself deep in your subconscious and conscious minds which will make it very hard for you to make a major change. People don't like their concept of you being challenged, especially if what you are trying to do is transformational. So be careful as you start to challenge your limiting beliefs about who you are and what you can be, do or have in this life because you WILL run into other people's beliefs and limiting expectations for you and like I said, even worse, you will run into *your own* limiting beliefs and expectations too. And you must not take their counsel. Not for one second. Turn away from any negativity or even what may seem like genuine concern and care for your wellbeing. Everyone is ultimately motivated by their own selfish needs and desires and your needs and desires are often not on their priority list. It's just the way it is, so steer clear of those who intend you no harm but also don't want to see you change into the human being you are completely capable of becoming.

Here is quick checklist for you to get started in changing some of your limiting beliefs. Ask yourself the following questions and complete the sentences below as honestly as you can:

1. Some of the strongest beliefs about my life and my emotions that I have which may be holding me back might are...
2. These beliefs began when I first....?
3. The reason I keep holding onto these beliefs is because...?
4. If I were to give up these beliefs, I would feel?
5. A belief which will serve me better could be?

Please, take the time to answer these questions. Sometimes all it takes is a new distinction, a new insight and a resolve to realise that a belief which has been holding you back is not actually as fixed and set in stone as you once believed it was. And *that* could be what makes all the difference to your life.

CHAPTER THREE

Self-discipline: A critical key to beating anxiety and depression

"It was character that got us about of bed, commitment that moved us into action and discipline that enabled us to follow through."

- Zig Ziglar

Self-discipline is a critical element in the journey to overcoming anxiety, depression and psychiatric drugs. Depending on where you are on the scale of depression, your levels of motivation and discipline can obviously be wildly different.

So, the first thing I want to say here is... I GET IT. Believe me, I know what it's like to not be able to scrounge up the desire to even have a shower or get yourself something to eat. When you're down there, there isn't going to be any discipline, motivation ...nothing. But it doesn't matter, and you want to know why?

Because you will get through it.

You need to know when you are stuck down there that you won't ALWAYS be stuck down there. Life is queer with its twists and turns, as a famous poem says. You don't know what is around the corner, what will happen tomorrow, who you will meet or connect with who may just be able to help lift you a little bit out of that deep, dark hole you're in. Allow time to heal, time to rest but be super aware that lying in bed or on the couch for hours and even days at a time is stealing your life way from you. It is also stopping you from creating the energy, motivation, changed state of mind, thinking and emotions that you need to get yourself out of anxiety and depression.

And so, having said that, it will be your ability to take little bits of consistent action in the different areas of your life – diet, exercise, reading, connecting – that will slowly but surely bring you back to life. And make no mistake about it: that is what we are doing here. Bringing you back to life. Your full and amazing life that is a gift beyond understanding to be enjoyed by you in all its magnificence.

The things I am going to suggest that you do here are not new to you but maybe you will see just how critical they are to your recovery because they are coming from someone who has been there, right down the rabbit hole, not just of anxiety or depression but of actually being trapped in drug-induced withdrawal every single time I tried to come off the antidepressants.

The discipline that I began to invoke in what I was doing began with researching exactly what the body needed to be fully supported to heal and produce its own serotonin. This began with taking a whole bag of supplements – consistently – every single day. Most people start taking a vitamin or supplement and then start to skip days or just stop taking them altogether. Because of my massive drive to beat anxiety and depression, I got motivated and disciplined and became amazingly consistent with this regimen.

I believe this did begin to make some great changes to the health and wellbeing of my body and mind but it was just the beginning, really. Ultimately, I don't think that we need that many supplements or vitamins because we can get most of what we need from our diet and it's actually what we eat, drink and do with our body and our mind that is the absolute key to beating anxiety, depression and overcoming and letting antidepressants go.

I will discuss my physical regimen and my eating habits in upcoming chapters so I won't focus on that here. This chapter is infinitely more important, because if you don't have the desire for your life to change it won't matter what I suggest you do. You might get a little motivation from me and decide to go for a walk around the block or even better, for a jog today, but without an unbelievably powerful *why* and the discipline to back that up, it's doubtful you will take it and "run with it" on your own and make it a *way of life*.

Make no mistake about it. What I am teaching you here is not a sometime thing. It is also not a "get out of jail free card" and then something you will do now and then when you feel better. It absolutely has to become *who you now are.* Forever. Does that a bit scary? Of course it is. Changing who we are and doing things which requires more of us is not easy. If it was, everyone would be disciplined. No one would have unhealthy habits which are causing them more trouble than they're worth. People wouldn't be stuck in their lives repeating the same behaviours and getting the same results which are not the results they want.

And the way I see it...is finding and maintaining the disciplined to do things which may be uncomfortable at first such a big price to pay? For your life, for your happiness, for your health, for your success, for your loved ones and for the contribution you *will* make to the world when you have beaten anxiety and depression?

It is also critical to not allow distraction from your main purpose. Distractions can be many in this life and especially these days with the lure of social media and trying to keep up with what everyone else is doing in their lives. Don't get caught up in that unless you're doing it for a very specific purpose like connecting with like-minded individuals who can encourage and support your growth and change.

If you are serious about changing your life for the better and moving out of anxiety and depression, you need to become absolutely watchful and ruthless about not only what you spend your life-time doing, but who you are doing it with and why. You need to be clear with regards to who around you actually deserve your time, energy and attention. So many of us don't seem to be aware and purposeful when it comes to this area of life and we all pay for it in terms of lost time and lost opportunities to learn, grow and achieve our desires and goals in life.

Other distractions may include dating, relationships, entertainment, the wrong kinds of hobbies, even certain social interactions with friends and family. You need to be very selective with your time, because you have a greater purpose to achieve here. This is not to say that you don't have time for relaxation or down time because ultimately, one of the most critical things you may need to learn to do on your journey to defeating anxiety and depression is to find the fun and laughter again. You may need to remember what it is that brings you the greatest sense of meaning, purpose and most of all JOY in your life.

Now, I know you are thinking that when you are in the state that you are in now that you can't enjoy anything at all. This is where people often tell me in counselling things like: "I am not enjoying anything that I used to enjoy. I seem to have lost the ability to enjoy ANYTHING, especially the things that I used to love the most". Believe me, I hear you and I know very well what this is like.

For example, one of my greatest enjoyments in life since I was a little boy has always been singing and listening to music and when I would begin to get stuck in depression that would be one of the first things to go. It would be one of the things I couldn't enjoy or connect with while in that deep, dark mental and emotional funk.

However, I encourage you to try, even if it's just for a few minutes at a time, and do your best to reconnect with the activities, the sights, the sounds, the sensations, and the smells that awaken your spirit. It is here, as you begin to feel better, that you will hook into being in the present moment and disconnecting from the negativity that is running rampant in your mind.

To do this as well as to get yourself to do SOME kind of exercise, meditation and any other basic routine you need to do to get better, you are going to need to love and discipline yourself with the greatest compassion and strength that you can possibly muster—as if your life depended on it…because it just might. So, it's time to get into gear – literally if you're going to be exercising! – and pick yourself up and start walking again. You can do this. I did it, over and over again, until I won and beat anxiety, depression and antidepressants. And of course, you will have bad days and setbacks. You *are* going to have days when you can't get out of bed and all you do is shuffle to the bathroom and maybe to the kitchen to get something to eat. I know. But keep the faith and get up tomorrow and discipline yourself to get outside and go for a walk. And then do it again the next day, and the next and the next. And then find something fun you used to do and go and do it. Pretend you're enjoying it at first. Read something inspirational if you can. Maybe you're reading this while you're stuck and I feel very privileged that you have chosen to listen to me rambling on when all you want to do is pull the covers over your head but I am telling you DON'T GIVE UP!

Discipline yourself but be compassionate at the same time

If you don't find a way to discipline yourself with love, you will create in yourself a fear of failure. By being hard on yourself, sometimes harder than anyone else would ever be, you are losing sight of an essential element of how to achieve your most cherished goals in life. If you do not treat yourself with compassion when you fall and when you fail, you will make "failing" so unbearable that you will eventually stop trying. This is also sometimes called "learned helplessness". It is a terrible, negative cycle.

This is, in fact, one of the techniques used to tame wild elephants in the circus. They tie the elephant with a rope to a very heavy pole. The elephant tries constantly to break away but can't and eventually stops trying. The pole is made lighter and lighter until the rope can just be tied to a small stick and the elephant won't bother trying to move it because it thinks any effort would be futile based on its past experience and conditioning.

It is likely that if you set yourself very high goals and do not achieve them as you had imagined or exactly on time, you are at risk of giving up too soon. You may, as I did, decide that failing to achieve some major lifelong and lofty goals by a certain age means you have failed. And if you have failed, then it is better not to set any further goals to avoid any future pain and disappointment. Better to just coast along and see what life brings you. But that would not serve you for very long.

Now, there is a time for coasting along or, if I put it another way, a time for letting go of the reins so tightly, building your trust in yourself, in life, in spirit and coming to a deep awareness that it is all happening perfectly and just as it should. As Esther Hicks is fond of saying when speaking for Abraham: "You can never get it wrong, and you will never get it done", because you are eternal and you didn't come here to "prove" that you can get it right. So sometimes we feel we have gotten it all wrong, that our lives have not worked out the way we hoped or wanted. And let me tell you something right now and I want you to pay very careful attention to what I am about to tell you:

Black Belt Mind

The greatest danger in your life is not that you may fail to achieve your greatest hopes, desires, dreams or goals. It is thinking that you have not and then giving up.

Now, I am not saying that having goals clearly written down and exact and according to some terribly overused acronym such as SMART isn't useful. It certainly is for some people. But not everyone is motivated in the same way and by the same things. Everyone has different fires burning in them and different ways of keeping those fires burning. That's the main thing, isn't it, in the end? Keeping the fire in you burning?

Sometimes it is perfectly fine to lose your way, because sometimes, as the saying goes, the only way to find yourself is to get lost. It is all part of the perfection of your journey. But, as I said above, the danger is that you lose your faith in yourself and the part that you have come to play on this earth and that is a great shame indeed. A great loss for humanity.

If Dr. Wayne Dyer had decided at the age of thirty-four that he was not going where he wanted to go and that his writing and his life were not worth pursuing, millions of people around the world would have lost out on his teachings and wisdom. Millions of people would not have been deeply touched by his words in his over forty-one books and countless talks and audio programmes. If he had decided that his failures meant more than his potential future success, we all would have lost. He had to learn to stand up and say, "I cheated on my first wife, I had some issues with alcohol and drugs, etc... but as I stand here before you today, all I know for sure is that I am better than I used to be, in every aspect of life that I can think of. A better man, a better father, a better writer and a better human being." These are more or less his words, which I have paraphrased.

Dr. Dyer passed away at the age of seventy-five, having written books and given lectures to millions of people across the world, bringing them comfort, peace of mind, inspiration and a new way to look at spirituality. What if Dr. Dyer had decided that he was not worthy of success because of some of his shortcomings and previous "failings"? What if he had not had the tenacity and mental discipline to keep his negative thoughts and emotions in check? And it would have taken bucket-loads of discipline to get himself to write nearly every day to produce over 41 books, not to mention audiobooks, speeches and other products that he created over his lifetime. His discipline became gifts to the world because if he had given up, nothing would have been produced and we would not all have learned what he most desired to teach us, and we all would have been "poorer" for it.

Do not get caught in the trap of thinking that your past equals your future. That is just an outright error in thinking and should have no place in your mindset. It certainly has no place for those who want to build a black belt mind. Failure is a part of success; they go hand in hand. As someone once said, if you haven't failed at something, you aren't trying hard enough.

Talent and Discipline

So many of us believe that those who succeed in life have some kind of higher-level talent than we do. We think that they were born with special gifts and abilities or privileges that helped them reach success. I am willing to concede that SOME people do succeed through certain inherited gifts. These may be genetic gifts – for example, the woman who is drop-dead gorgeous who also has a knack for singing and dancing and goes onto super-stardom based on those "inherited" gifts of genetics. However, just as many reach the same heights of success without having those kinds of advantages to begin with.

There are also those who were born into money and were therefore not only given the financial backing to launch their successes but they were also surrounded by role models who understood money and shared their understanding with them.

However, there are multitudes more of those who started with nothing or less than nothing, in debt, downcast, and with few contacts and little understanding of money or how to make it, who took their destiny into their own hands and succeeded.

With any level of success, regardless of whether someone inherited an advantage or whether they fought tooth and nail for every little scrap of success along the way, there was ALWAYS discipline.

You can have the greatest talent, financial backing, genetic makeup or social influence in the world but if you don't have the discipline to wake up in the morning and BRING IT, and to overcome setbacks, and to push through obstacles and disappointments and disruptions to your plans and progress, then you cannot hope to succeed.

This applies just the same to your desire to be free from anxiety and depression—even more so. Why? Because your mental and physical ability to be disciplined can be severely compromised and hijacked by the misty, murky landscape of negativity, lethargy and fear that can grip you tightly and not let you go.

In the beginning, you will need to build your discipline muscles slowly, just as you are going to need to build up your actual physical muscles and fitness levels. In order to begin to break the negative cycle of low energy, negative thinking and inaction you are going to need to start with a spark. That spark is digging deeper than you have ever before to find your WHY. Why do you want to come out of anxiety and depression and break these bonds holding you back from who you really are deep down?

Who needs you to beat your anxiety and depression? Who is relying on you? I don't care if there is no one obvious who comes to mind, there are people out there suffering right now just as you are who need your help. They need you to get past this and then to go and find them and lift them up too. There is no greater reward for doing this work than what you get to do for others once you have recovered and the impact you can have when you have shown yourself every day that you are greater than anxiety and depression.

Read this and brand it in your brain forever:

Failure cannot cope with persistence

Write it out or print it out and stick it on your walls, your cupboards, your fridge and your bathroom mirrors.

Your capability as a human being to be resilient and to be persistent in taking a step every day – any step – towards beating back anxiety and depression is infinite, just as long as you DON'T GIVE UP. You can trip, you can fall, you can cry, you can scream, you can rage, you can stay in bed today. But by God, you're going to get up tomorrow and you're going to BRING IT.

And then, as you take that first step, you will see the next one light up in front of you, and then the next and then the next.

You will be led to information, people, experiences and knowledge that you had no idea even existed. And as you learn and grow and take these steps, you will find that your ability to stay on track gets stronger—and not only stronger but easier too!

When I began to discipline myself to run nearly every single morning at around 5:15 am, what I discovered after doing this for a period of about three months was that my fitness levels kept increasing and as that happened I began to notice that even though the distances I was running were getting further and further, my ability to handle them was getting increasingly easier. I almost couldn't believe the exponential leaps in fitness I began to experience purely through the discipline of doing something on an almost daily basis. It was something I had never experienced before when I was running only two or three times a week.

There are rewards beyond your imagination waiting for you when you decide that discipline is not painful. Discipline is not stifling for your life or your lifestyle. In fact, discipline will set you freer than you have ever hoped to be. And it will literally give you not only your life back if you are suffering with anxiety, depression and antidepressants but it will lead you to a version of yourself you never even dreamed was possible.

CHAPTER FOUR

It's all about energy

"Nothing happens until something moves."

– Albert Einstein

Everything in this universe is energy-based. Energy is found in every conceivable element of the physical-material as well as the mental-spiritual universe. Energy is what sustains life on this planet, whether it is energy from the sun, the sea, movement of water and wind farms, or a gentle breeze of air that blows into a confined space.

At one of the smallest possible levels of life we know that if we split an atom we can generate enough "energy" to destroy the earth. At the largest levels of our physical existence, if our planet didn't continue to have the "energy" to move around the sun, we would all have perished a long time ago. The energy required for our planet to move through space and circle the sun on a predetermined and somewhat magically perfect circumference is something that nearly all of us take for granted every morning when we get up and see that the sun has "come up" again.

As energy-driven manifestations, we humans rely on energy for our life force, and there are many sources we can derive our energy from. It can be from the sun, food, drink, movement, and the very cells of our own body and mind.

When our energy is balanced and we are generating enough energy for our needs, we feel satisfied. We feel happy, joyous, connected and able to do all the things that we need or want to do on a daily basis.

However, if something has gone wrong in our energy supply or the expression and use of our energy, then things can go very wrong indeed.

Just as electricity – which is an intense form of energy – has the power to be life giving, life supporting and healing, it also has the power to take life away…sometimes very quickly. We all know that we need to show respect for electricity and we don't go around putting our fingers into light sockets or outlets just to see what would happen if we tapped into "too much energy".

We also feel it when that electricity is suddenly absent from our lives. We cannot cook or warm our food. We cannot heat our water or warm our bodies in the middle of winter and we cannot see where we are going when night falls. And it can be a little dangerous wandering around in the dark with all those bedside cabinets lurking with their pointy edges just waiting for us to stub our toes on.

This analogy is perfect to explain my theory on how the way that energy is generated, used and expressed in the human body and mind has the power to heal and the power to destroy.

We must show a much greater respect for and awareness of how energy enters into our bodies through the foods we eat, the activities we do and…strangely enough…the company we keep.

Most people wouldn't really give much notice to the effect that different people in their lives have on their energy levels – both mental (psychic) and physical (body). However, if you were to ask just about anyone you know whether some people help them feel energised whilst others seem to "drain" their energy, I'm pretty much willing to bet they would all say absolutely yes. We have *all* had this experience from time to time. If you're a human being and you've lived even a little bit of life you have had the experience of some people being energy givers or creators and others being energy takers. When we allow these people to remain in our own mental, emotional and physical space for any period of time (that could be merely a few minutes in some cases!), we are at risk of having our own daily store of energy drained right out of us. What does this actually do to us?

It causes a physical and mental lowering of whatever energy we have been able to generate and makes whatever else we needed that energy for less possible on that day. This is, in effect, tantamount to allowing people to steal from us.

This is different to being supportive of someone who is struggling and has come to you for your help. Their energy levels may very well be low but they have acknowledged this and have asked for you to share some of your energy with them and then you get to choose whether that is something you are willing to do.

When it is also happens to be your profession and calling that may be different again as we have to allow people to enter into our space and know that there may be an impact on our own psychic and physical energy reserves for that day. Anyone who has ever been a counsellor or therapist will attest to this and knows that there is a limit to how many people you can or should see in any given day. When I worked as a contracted psychologist to an employee assistance programme for about five years we were expected to do six hours of counselling per day. That is usually manageable but I don't think it's sustainable five days per week. At one stage, because I desperately needed the money and because they paid so poorly, I did seven counselling sessions every Tuesday, and those were also the days when I would go straight from all that counselling to having my kids because that was my night with them after I got divorced. I used to joke with people who tried to call or message me on those nights that even if God called me on those particular evenings I wouldn't answer him either!

After five years of doing this, plus having no ability to take sick leave (because I was a contractor), plus no annual leave – and so I wasn't able to take a holiday with my kids for five years – and seeing approximately 30 people per week for an hour of counselling each with a range of issues including anxiety, depression, phobias, marital issues, relationship breakdowns, grief and a whole range of other difficulties, I just crashed.

To this day I don't even know how I lasted as long as I did, and that was on top of some other major difficulties that I experienced during that time of my life. My body and mind just couldn't sustain that level of energy drain happening on such a consistent basis, plus the drain that comes from major stress (financial), emotional upsets (relationship breakdowns) and physical-biological stress on the brain and body (antidepressant withdrawal).

This is when I hit rock bottom and had to either do something to change my life or probably leave this world. I chose the first option because I made the firm decision one day that it wouldn't be me who would decide when the time had come for me to leave this earth. And I couldn't bear the thought of what it would do to my children. What I was going through was already hard on them and the guilt was just killing me, but leaving them was going to make things much worse…or at least that's what I told myself, and thank God I had that to hold onto.

What I did next was what started to turn it all around for me. I decided that I needed to get the hell out of that cycle of working as a contracted psychologist and being paid a pittance for the volume and intensity of work I was delivering.

Don't get me wrong. I absolutely loved working with my clients and I loved being able to help them improve their lives and alleviate so much of their mental and emotional suffering. In my time with that particular employee assistance provider I had also become the resident couples' counsellor because most of the other psychologists didn't want to touch couples' counselling. They found it too intense, grueling at times and seldom rewarding. However, I did and I still do find couples' counselling intriguing, challenging and very rewarding.

Most of my clients made use of their full session allowance, which was usually around six sessions that their employer covered, and many of them asked for extensions for another one or two as well. I took this to be a good sign that the work we were doing was helping them and I often got that immediate feedback from the clients. So the work itself was intrinsically rewarding even if the organisation refused to recognise or reward the work that was being done on their behalf for their customers.

However, as I mentioned, I couldn't sustain that level of giving of my energy. I was helping everyone else and thought I was doing the only thing I could do at the time, which was to keep working in a relatively "stable" income environment doing work I loved, but I was paying an awful price when it came to my mental and physical health. My energy levels were being depleted just as quickly as my body and mind were attempting to restore them. And mostly there was more energy going out than coming in. This is not a state of existence that the mind and body can maintain for a long period of time before things start to go wrong. And the certainly began to go wrong for me but I just kept pushing through because I didn't know what else to do. I did it for five years which was on the back of an even longer period of personal and professional difficulty that I experienced from the time I arrived in Australia right through to 2010 when I began contract counselling to pay the bills.

I believe that I what experienced at that time was burnout. In addition, I was beginning to experience what is known as compassion fatigue. It came to a point where I was hoping the clients wouldn't show up. It came to a point where I was so depleted that I had nothing left to give and I certainly wasn't giving to myself. I knew that if that was how I was feeling then I was getting to the point of not being able to be of service to my clients anymore.

It was also towards the end of that period that the requests for help were coming in thick and fast from those who had read my 2013 story of how I managed to get off antidepressants the first time. Whilst I offered whatever I could to everyone who wrote to me, I knew I had to pull right back and go away for a while.

I came very close to leaving the field of psychology and counselling altogether because I just couldn't see how I could earn enough in full time employment as a psychologist to cover all my expenses as a single dad to three kids, living in Sydney – one of the most expensive cities in the world to live in. Believe me, if I could have packed up and left to live in a cheaper part of the city, country or even the world, I would have done it. But my ex-wife and my daughter's mum would never have gone to the same place and then I would not be able to see my children and that just wasn't an option for me.

So I found a job working as a student counsellor for one of the largest colleges in Australia. It was a one-year contract and it was an hour travel by car from where I lived but I didn't care. It provided me with the ability to reassess where I was in life and what direction I wanted to go in while still counselling and providing help to students of all ages and backgrounds who were very appreciative of the help I provided to them. During that time, I worked with a wonderful senior counsellor and we were both sad to part ways after my one year with the college ended and I moved on to working for another employee assistance provider as a senior clinician and trainer. The balance that I found at the new provider and the amazingly supportive team was just the right mix for me.

The point of the story is that my time at TAFE allowed me the space to recover from the ordeal of the previous five years. However, it was also during my drives to work every morning and evening that I had the time and space to reconnect to the work of Dr. Wayne

Dyer as well as Esther Hicks through listening to audiobooks, podcasts and YouTube videos. This was certainly a big part of what helped me not only recover from the burnout but it also was integral in setting me on the path that would eventually lead me to finally beating back anxiety and depression and getting off antidepressants for good.

I progressively healed myself and began to find my health and happiness once again. And with it came a renewal of desire and energy to help others and share what I had learned and finally cemented for myself in terms of wellbeing.

My time and space became extremely precious to me after that. I removed negative, energy-draining influences from my life (including a somewhat toxic friendship), and I began to meditate almost every day. I had already changed to a predominantly gluten-free diet in 2016 but I didn't start my current exercise and dietary regimen until late 2017 when everything moved to a completely different level for me.

As I began to protect and nurture my energy – mental, physical and spiritual – I began to get stronger.

I believe that when it comes to our mental and physical health, everything is connected to either a deficiency or an oversupply of energy. And so, we must ask what actually produces an "energetic" reaction in the brain? When it comes to the mental phenomena in our minds, we can usually point towards the neurotransmitter family—dopamine, serotonin and norepinephrine—and indeed, these are the brain messengers that the antidepressant drugs attempt to artificially increase in our bodies and brains.

Dopamine is the neurotransmitter that is connected to learning, memory, reward, sensation, motivation, pleasure, focus and attention. We know that some psychological conditions such as schizophrenia have been linked to an oversupply of dopamine in the brain. Too much energy leads to an overflow of information and too many signals being fired off indiscriminately.

Too little dopamine and we may end up suffering from debilitating conditions such as Parkinson's disease, and there is some belief that lowered levels of dopamine can also lead to the development of ADHD (attention deficit disorder). However, just as with the serotonin neurotransmitter, there are many natural ways to balance this out that do not require dangerous "medications" – which according to one of the largest longitudinal studies (200 patients over 15 years) completed on schizophrenia patients who had been on antipsychotics led to increased brain damage through reduction in brain matter (Andreasen et al., 2013).[3]

Let us now look briefly at some of the symptoms of anxiety and depression and see if there is a logical and intuitive connection between those two very different – yet related – conditions and energy systems in the mind and body.

The energy connection with anxiety and depression

When we think about anxiety we sometimes refer to a person as having "nervous energy" and when we think of depression we refer to someone struggling with "lethargy", both descriptors of either an excitable state of energy in the human body and mind or as a lowered and "depressed" level of mental and/or physical energy or activity.

When people get stressed or anxious their mind and body go into overdrive, producing symptoms such as increased heart rate, sweating, racing thoughts, tense muscles and a general state of excessive energy. An anti-anxiety drug works by interfering with the neurons that are firing in reaction to a perceived threat. The adrenal system is also overworking, pumping adrenaline and cortisol into the body in preparation for a fight. However, in most cases these days, we are not in imminent mortal danger. Our stressors tend to

---

[3] Andreasen et al, 2013. Dept. of Psychosis Studies, Kings College, London.

be mostly mentally conceived but they can be prolonged through ongoing attention to the source of the perceived threat to our well-being. Over time, it's like an engine overheating or revving too high for too long...eventually it will burn itself out because it's not a stable or balanced state to be in.

And so, what does the stressed or anxious person need to do? They need to settle the whole system down. How?
On a physical level, one of the very first things I teach anyone who comes to me with anxiety is to learn how to breath and rebalance the oxygen to carbon dioxide that is entering and exiting their system. As our brain perceives a threat it will take over the breathing apparatus and cause us to take short and shallow breaths, preparing for action. This contraction leads to a tension in the body and is a feedback loop between our brains and body, signaling that we need to react and do something to stop the danger. However, most of the time we aren't even really aware of what it is that is causing us to feel so anxious, as some of it sits below the surface of our subconscious minds.

Luckily, we have the full ability to regain control of our breathing from the autonomic nervous system and begin to slow it down by taking slow and deep breaths in through the nose and out through the mouth, counting four seconds in and four seconds out. After approximately one to three minutes of doing this the brain gets the message that there is no danger and it stops reacting. And as we breathe longer and then focus for a few minutes on the body, letting go of any tension in the muscles and joints, the brain further settles down. Continuing with this for another few minutes and actively letting all thoughts go then leads to our mind and body relaxing and letting go of the energy that was being over-produced. This also helps to ensure enough energy is available for the other things we need to do that day.

That was a simple explanation of only one tool to bring the level of activation down and rebalance our nervous energy. We will discuss meditation more specifically in chapter seven.

Unfortunately, most people think this is too simple and don't even really try it long enough and consistently enough to get the kinds of results that would absolutely prove to them the power of this simple technique to revolutionise their wellbeing.

Most tend to go see the doctor, who prescribes some kind of medication, sleep tablet or in some cases a benzodiazepine such as Valium or Xanax, which are not just a Band-Aid to the real issue but also an extremely difficult trap that millions of people across the world are falling into.

When it comes to depression, the opposite is true. Here we find that the thoughts that people experience are lower energy thoughts. They are usually very negative and global in nature (meaning the person is seeing their life in very absolute and mostly unfair terms). The system begins to slow with depression; thinking slows too and then the person experiences a distinct lack of energy in mind, emotion and physical activity. Unfortunately, as I mentioned in the previous chapter, it is a huge trap that people fall into, not realising that the desire to rest and sleep and withdraw is exactly the opposite of what will help them feel better. The system is down and it's stuck in a very low energy state. The body and brain are either under-producing serotonin or there may be something else interfering with the serotonin production. As you will see in the upcoming chapter, it may something as simple as an antibiotic that is interfering with serotonin production or it may be a much more complex combination of factors that include negative thinking patterns, lowered physical activity (leading to lowered energy in the body and mind), lowered intake of energy-producing foods and a lack of social connection (which also assists with elevating energy levels).

On thinking about the methods we can use to increase our energy levels in the body and brain, the ideal route to restoring our mental and physical health is to focus on each major aspect of our lives as described above and then ensure that we are bringing as much natural and life-giving energy to the body and mind as possible. Doing whatever we can to assist our bodies to produce and provide us with all the positive and life-affirming energy that we need should be our primary focus if we want to elevate ourselves out of anxiety or depression.

We need to support the body with the right nutritious food and drinks (mostly water) that not only produce optimal energy but that don't detract or unbalance our body's natural ability to produce and manage its own energy levels. This is critical to ensuring our overall mental, physical, and ultimately spiritual well-being

CHAPTER FIVE

Food for Thought

"Let food be thy medicine."

– Hippocrates

The information in this chapter may at first seem too simple to be a potential recovery strategy for something as global and seemingly intractable as the epidemic of stress, anxiety and depression that the world seems to be facing at the moment.

However, we humans love to complicate things, don't we? We all know some of the answers and ideas that you are about to read in this chapter...not all of them...but a lot of them will be familiar to you, I am sure. I had also come across some of them before in my tireless quest to find out what works to heal anxiety and depression.

However, many of the things you will read about here will be quite new and possibly even surprising to you, as they were for me as I dove deep into what we need to do from a nutritional point of view to help reverse anxiety and depression.

Since publishing the first part of my story online and because I provided my contact details to readers, I have received hundreds of emails from people from all over the world for the past five years asking for guidance either for themselves or for a loved one, whether it is a parent, child, sibling or friend.

These people are often at a loss, confused, afraid and wondering where to turn for help. A consistent theme that comes up is their frustration with the medical professional who is either treating them or their loved one. This is because when the issue of the drug being the problem or a tapering off is suggested, these medical professionals respond with anything from indifference to outright hostility towards their patients or suggest that they need to try another medication or take an additional one to stop the side effects of the first one!

This is not a just a couple of people who experience this reaction, this is a percentage of the world's population who are being put on anti-depressant medications for very different reasons without any thought as to whether medications are the right path to take or what the potential impact could be if the patient did have to take them and then couldn't stop taking them because of antidepressant withdrawal issues.

With regards to diet, what I am primarily focusing on here is what is believed to be the key issue when it comes to anxiety and depression, and that is lowered levels of serotonin and the brain and body's ability to communicate effectively using the neurotransmitters we need to help us cope and feel good in life. These lowered levels may come about for a variety of reasons, as will be discussed, and what I propose is a dietary approach and a vitamin and supplement approach that are targeted at both increasing the actual levels of serotonin in the body and brain as well as increasing and facilitating the body and the brain's capacity to communicate effectively within itself.

So many doctors and psychiatrists know little or nothing about some of the things I am going to talk about in this chapter with regards to exactly what produces serotonin and dopamine in our bodies and brains, or how our bodies convert certain foods, supplements and amino acids into our happy, peaceful and energising neurotransmitters – dopamine, serotonin and noradrenalin.

At the time when I first managed to get off antidepressants in 2013, I actually knew very little about the dietary requirements or changes that some people probably need to implement in order to really create and sustain a significant shift in their physiology, thinking, emotions, energy, and therefore their capacity to overcome anxiety and depression.

In 2014 things fell apart – again – when my daughter's mother and I split up and I made a career move that really didn't fit with who I truly am or what I really love to do. And it was then that I first received an idea or insight from a reader of my story on the Mad in America website. He mentioned that some people use something called 5-HTP to help them recover from depression after they stop taking antidepressants. I was intrigued and decided to do a little digging into what 5-HTP is. I will describe exactly what it is later in this chapter but suffice to say for now that it opened my eyes to the fact that there is not only a medically driven model of how we can increase neurotransmitters in our bodies and our brains and we have been "brainwashed" into thinking only pharmaceutical interventions will help to alleviate the suffering of anxiety and depression.

Following on from that discovery, I decided to research everything that I could about how to naturally increase the key neurotransmitters that were supposedly involved in mental health and wellbeing.

As I researched further I found that there were amino acid supplements which could be taken to help elevate some of our other neurotransmitters. For example, L-Tyrosine is a naturally occurring amino acid which is available as a relatively inexpensive food supplement that can assist in increasing both dopamine and norepinephrine.

Dopamine is the neurotransmitter in our bodies and brains that provides the sensations and emotions related to pleasure and enjoyment. Norepinephrine and epinephrine are involved in increasing adrenaline and therefore our energy, drive and motivation levels. They obviously play an important part in our survival when we are under attack and having unusually low levels would be indicative of fatigue and even depression.

This would explain why pharmacologists and the pharmaceutical companies thought they were being clever by adding noradrenaline reuptake inhibitors to some of the new antidepressants such as Effexor, Pristiq and Cymbalta, which are called SNRIs (serotonin and noradrenaline reuptake inhibitors).

Once again, this leads to the same problem that I mentioned before because this is *artificially* increasing these neurotransmitters in your brain. It doesn't actually create *more* of them. It just screws with your brain's process of taking some of the neurotransmitters back that haven't been used in a process of signaling messages and effectively dams up the synapse which leads to more of the neurotransmitter floating around and eventually firing off more signals. This obviously causes some immediate side effects as well as longer term issues as your brain and body continually need to adjust to this foreign substance interfering with its natural processes.

When you take an amino acid supplement you are actually *increasing* the volume of those neurotransmitters available for use by your body and brain. You are doing it naturally and you are not going to experience major problems "getting onto them" and then hell when you feel life has improved and it's time to stop taking them. They do not, as far as I am aware, have any withdrawal syndromes like the antidepressants do. I will provide specific detail about these amino acids further on in this chapter but for now let's look at how various foods and other medications could be part of the difficulties we experience with anxiety and depression.

Sugar

One of the very first things that I gave up on my journey to reclaiming my wellbeing was sugar. I never had much of a sweet tooth throughout my life. I think I have always had more of a savory pallet; however, I do like the occasional chocolate and ice cream and to this day I would never deprive myself of that pleasure in life. However, I did for a period of time insist to myself that I needed to at least keep my one spoon of raw sugar for my morning coffee. I don't believe in the deprivation method to anything in life. I don't think it's sustainable for most people anyway.

However, I pretty much dropped all sugar from my diet, which started off with no sugar-filled foods or drinks such as fizzy drinks and even fruit juices. If I did have fruit juice it would be something like watered-down apple juice, which is also something I insist on with my kids. I eventually progressed to dropping even that one spoon of raw sugar in my morning coffee – which I had sworn I would never do!

The reason that sugar is such a culprit for anxiety and depression is that it elevates your blood sugar levels *artificially* (seeing a pattern here?) and it is very short-lived and then throws your system into deprivation pretty quickly. So you have the "sugar high", as people like to call it, and feel energised and then you drop like a stone, and you crash and burn. And what does this do to your mind, body, and your emotions? You know the answer to that.

Removing sugar was almost a no-brainer and it wasn't that hard for me. I can almost hear your groans and protests already:

"I can't give up sugar!" "I can't give up my chocolate...it's my greatest pleasure in life!" "I can't give up sugar in my coffee!"

Well, I am here to tell you that you CAN and in fact, you MUST give up the unnatural and ADDED sugars to your diet. What I mean by "unnatural" is any sugar that does not directly come from a food i.e. processed and refined sugars. Fruit is fine and the sugar in fruit is known as sucrose and that is fine of course...in moderation. Even then, I don't tend to eat a lot of fruit these days aside from apples and some nectarines in summer. Certain fruits such as orange juice will spike your blood sugar levels very quickly and so you need to be careful of this. Just give two cups of orange or apple juice to a five year old and see what happens! Does the term "bouncing off the walls" come to mind? It certainly does for me and then I wonder if that is what it does to the kids, what is it doing to us even though we are bigger and the effects may not be as immediate or obvious?

You really want your body to begin producing all of its own energy from your day to day diet. You do not need any additional sugar from anywhere. You will get plenty of glucose from eating a balanced diet – unless, of course, you have a condition like diabetes, but I am not referring to anyone who has a specific medical issue with glucose.

Gluten

What exactly is gluten?

According to international bestselling author Dr. David Perlmutter, gluten derives from the word glue. Why? Because it is used in a range of foods and products in order to BIND products together. It is what holds your cookie together and also gives it its soft, plastic and stretchy texture. This is why some gluten free products can feel a bit hard but if you find a good product or brand they can get around that issue pretty easily these days.

So, why would it be bad for you to ingest something that has a "glue-like" structure to it? Pretty obvious, isn't it? Imagine what your stomach has to do to break that down and also what your liver has to do to process it and then what your kidneys have to do to get rid of it!

According to Dr. Perlmutter, who has spent over 30 years researching the kind of impact that certain food additives have on our bodies and our brains, gluten causes *inflammation* in the body.

It is fairly easy for us to observe or sense the kind of inflammation it causes in the body with things like arthritis, gout and skin inflammations. However, more subtle, sinister and unnoticeable is the inflammation that it causes in our brains.

You see, the brain itself doesn't have any nerve endings. We cannot feel damage to the brain as we can feel damage to the body. So if the brain is getting inflamed on a fairly regular basis, we don't really notice but some of the impacts of that inflammation in the brain can exacerbate or even cause anxiety and depression.

People who are celiac have a much higher level of intolerance to gluten and can suffer from debilitating abdominal conditions if they mistakenly eat it.

I believe everyone has some level of intolerance to gluten because the body just struggles to process, digest and get rid of it. When we eat gluten-filled products, we are making our organs work very hard to clear, cleanse and repair themselves every single day. Your body – and your mind – can only do that for so long before something starts to break down.

Back in 2008, I went to see a naturopath because I was struggling with a skin condition. Mostly, I was struggling with some redness and flaking around my nose and forehead. Nothing I did seemed to improve this. I could drink as much water as I wanted. I could run three times a week and try sweating it out and whilst this did help to a certain degree, nothing really worked to improve this horrible and often highly embarrassing skin condition.

When I would get more stressed, of course, or if I had a run of not sleeping well, it would flare up as well and get worse too. But I found regardless of whether things were going smoothly or stressfully, the skin condition persisted.

When I went to see the naturopath, she did some kind of test on me. I don't recall if it was a skin reaction test or something similar, but she told me that I was quite sensitive to gluten and that I should try dropping all gluten for a few weeks and see what would happen.

To be honest, I thought she was a bit flaky but I thought I would give it a try. In those days (only ten years ago), there weren't that many gluten-free products in the supermarkets at all. And the cost of one (disgustingly small) loaf of gluten-free bread was enough to make you swallow hard before pulling out your debit card!

I bought it, though, and I also tried some gluten-free pasta, which was just terrible. I then tried to avoid other gluten products but to be honest, I really didn't follow through on it and so I had no idea whether it would help me or not. Life was hard back then with the birth of our second child and at that stage, our marriage was already beginning to fail. I was quite miserable and didn't really have the motivation or the drive to make a gluten-free life stick.

Fast forward to 2016 and the world has changed. Gluten-free products are EVERYWHERE and the relative price of a gluten-free, delicious loaf of seeded bread is almost the same price as regular bread. There are pasta options just as good (actually better) than the regular gluten filled ones. I made a decision after reading Dr. Perlmutter's book to stop gluten altogether. Now, again, I don't believe in the complete deprivation process of making dietary changes in one's life because I don't think living in that state of withholding and deprivation is good for anyone and it won't lead to long term and permanent changes in habits and ways of living. So I still have the odd piece of cake on occasion at a birthday party but I would say I have a 90% gluten-free diet.

One of the very first things I noticed after being "gluten free" for about four weeks was that my skin condition completely disappeared. After years and years of trying to sort this embarrassing condition out it just went away! This was encouraging, of course, but it also gave me pause to wonder if gluten was causing inflammation like that with my skin, what exactly was it doing inside my body in other places and of course in my brain – just as Dr. Perlmutter states in *Grain Brain?* Well, I decided if nothing else, I was going to keep up the gluten-free diet because my body obviously didn't respond well to gluten, regardless of what it may or may not have been contributing to my mental health struggles.

Now, I cannot tell you definitively that the gluten-free diet led to major improvements in my mental state but it is uncanny that if I were to pinpoint when things started to change and improve for me it was around that time. Going gluten free was just a step on the path, however, and I was doing A LOT of other work on my thinking, my perception of my life and what things mean to me, and I also made some much-needed changes to the levels of stress I was experiencing through the setup of the work I was doing at the time. Many of the things I did and still do are in the other chapters of this book.

Antibiotics

It came as quite a surprise to me whilst reading Dr. Perlmutter's work to learn that anyone who has had to take antibiotics for a period of time may have lowered levels of serotonin due to the fact that antibiotics – which most of us know destroy good and bad bacteria in the gut – destroy and prevent the creation of serotonin in our stomachs as well.

As I was pondering this it suddenly occurred to me that when I turned 15 years old I got a really bad attack of acne. I tried all the soaps and just about anything I could to stop it but it just went from bad to worse. It didn't help that I had recently got braces and glasses as well, and so my self-esteem suffered terribly during my teen years.

However, I remembered that rather than prescribing Roaccutane, the skin specialist recommended another acne medication called Minocycline. As an aside, the brand name Accutane (Roaccutane) was discontinued by its manufacturer, Roche, in 2009. A 2001 article in the New England Journal of Medicine linked Accutane to depression. A U.S. Food and Drug Administration (FDA) study examined 110 people who took Accutane and were hospitalized for depression or attempted suicide. Their ages ranged from 12 to 47.

The FDA (Food and Drug Administration) had received over 431 reported cases of depression, suicidal ideation, suicide attempts or suicide in patients treated with isotretinoin (Accutane). There were 37 patients who committed suicide, 24 of them while using it and 13 after ceasing to use it; 31 of them were male with a median age of just 17. A history of mental health issues was only reported prior to starting the drug in eight of the cases. Accutane was at that stage reported to be in the top 10 drugs in the FDA database in terms of the reports of the numbers of depression and suicide attempts while being on or after coming off the drug.

Although it was clearly not as powerful as Accutane, I took Minomycin (Minocycline) religiously as a teenager for approximately four years, trying to settle and clear the uncomfortable and highly embarrassing acne that I had started to experience.

I recently decided to look it up online and was surprised to learn that it is a broad-spectrum antibiotic! Every day... for four years...as a teenager. If what Dr. Perlmutter says is true, and I have no reason to doubt his credentials or over thirty years of research into the food brain connection, then my brain was being starved of essential neurotransmitters during a crucial time in my adult development. This is because, as Dr. Perlmutter clearly explains, antibiotics don't just destroy good and bad bacteria in the gut; they also break down serotonin production. And we now know that most of the body's serotonin is not produced in the brain at all but in the gut. Logically...where else could it be produced?

Now, I am not saying that it was exclusively the reason that I struggled with anxiety in my young adult life (although on thinking about it I do not remember being an anxious child or prepubescent). In fact, I was quite a little risk taker and would often land myself in hot water at home for jumping off roofs, almost killing myself flying down a street on my BMX bicycle with no brakes, throwing fruit over the fence and smashing my best friend's neighbour's window or smoking behind an old oak tree at the age of 10 or so. I was naughty and I clearly didn't get anxious about taking risks.

So when I reflected on taking antibiotics for all those years and then seeing in black and white that they can either destroy or prevent serotonin from being produced in the stomach, it really gave me pause to rethink just exactly where my anxiety in my late teens and early twenties had come from. Nature, nurture or something much worse.... medical science in the form of drugs supposed to help us...but unwittingly doing more damage than they are worth. This is just the tip of the iceberg. It really makes me wonder how many teenagers are suffering needlessly from anxiety and/or depression due to this issue. Going through puberty is hard enough without antibiotics screwing up your neurobiology!

What I am really trying to get across here is just to be aware that if you are taking antibiotics, you MAY have a problem with lowered levels of serotonin and dopamine and as such it is just good practice to take a high potency probiotic. Dr. Perlmutter recommends in particular that you ensure that the bacteria bifidobacterium infantis is present in your probiotic.

This next section will detail some of the most important vitamins, minerals and amino acids that you can take to assist you in staying away from taking anti-depressants in the first place, feeling better while being on them or supporting you during a tapering programme. This has been, as I mentioned earlier, a four-year odyssey for me both personally and professionally as I have tried various options as I learned about them, avoided others due to fear-mongering online (only to find out there were other reasons certain amino acids were not commercially available), and am still in the process of investigating some others.

What I have learned and shared with my clients and those who write to me from all over the world has helped many people cope better with anti-depressant and anti-anxiety drug withdrawal. When I think of the needless suffering that hundreds and thousands of people have gone through across the globe due to a lack of understanding and awareness of other viable alternatives to taking psychiatric medication for anxiety and depression I get pretty fired up, as you could possibly tell from my writing. The number of young teens being put on anti-anxiety and/or anti-depressant drugs, prematurely in some cases and completely unnecessarily in other cases, makes me really angry. As they say, if only I knew then what I know now, and if I could magically have gone back in time to my 23-year-old self back in March 2000, I could have possibly saved myself 17 years of the difficulties of being on and trying to come off these medications. It's not only what I have had to go through but what my family and some friends have had to go through too, and I know I am certainly not alone when it comes to not only the antidepressants but mental health in general when people struggle with anxiety and/or depression.

So here is a summary of the vitamins, minerals and other supplements which have the potential to help you with anxiety and depression in the most natural manner possible:

5-HTP (5- Hydroxytryptophan)

As mentioned before, 5 HTP was the first supplement that was brought to my attention very soon after I published my story online in 2013 by one of the readers of the story. This particular person mentioned that once off the medications, some people have used an amino acid called 5-HTP. I had never, not once in thirteen years of experiencing anxiety and depression personally or as a mental health professional, heard about 5-HTP. Have you heard of it? I'm willing to bet that you haven't and that your doctor and definitely your psychiatrist haven't either. Why is that? What is 5-HTP?

5-HTP is a chemical by-product of the protein building block L-tryptophan. It is also produced commercially (and this is what you would be taking if you chose to try it) from the seeds of an African plant known as Griffonia simplicifolia. 5-HTP is the last step in the process of converting protein in your stomach into the essential neurotransmitters – serotonin and dopamine. Protein is the key building block required in your diet which your body uses to synthesize (using a combination of vitamins) into L-tryptophan and then 5-HTP. Having high levels of 5-HTP should lead to higher levels of serotonin and dopamine, which should lead you to feel calmer, happier, more focused and generally more optimistic. Note that it can take a number of weeks to be effective and – once again – the dosage is variable (a typical dose of 5-HTP is in the range of 100-300mg, taken either once daily or in divided doses. 5-HTP is used as a supplement (rather than tryptophan itself) to increase serotonin levels because tryptophan can be diverted into niacin production or protein construction whereas 5-HTP has the sole fate of serotonin synthesis. 5-HTP also crosses the blood brain barrier easily.[4]

Although this may seem like a scary way to approach taking something to help with anxiety or depression, I would prefer trying various dosages of 5-HTP any day over playing around with an anti-depressant or anti-anxiety medication. It's certainly, in my opinion, worth trying the 5-HTP first to see if it can provide some benefit. Of course, it won't work for everyone and this is why one of the upcoming chapters in this book is about you questioning everything and everyone...including me! Please do be aware that 5-HTP can cause some discomfort in the stomach and if you are struggling with this you may just need to discontinue it. When I have taken it at night I haven't had any issues.

Even though it is becoming more widely known that the chemical imbalance theory of mental health problems has never been completely proven, these neurotransmitters *do* exist and are most likely *part* of the cause of many of the cases of clinical depression and

---

[4] https://examine.com/supplements/5-htp/

debilitating anxiety (and in some cases panic attacks) that people struggle with.

However, it is one thing to say that serotonin levels have been lowered, possibly caused by stressful life events which led to increased cortisol – a chemical in the body released during times of stress which may also reduce production of serotonin in the body – but it is quite another thing to tell a person that he or she has a "chemical imbalance" in their brain and that they therefore have some sort of "disease" that is as incurable as diabetes.

"Just keep taking your medications the same way a diabetic needs insulin" and shut up and don't you dare challenge the established order of psychiatry's control of medicating anxiety and depression. And don't worry about the kickbacks and links between some doctors and others in the psychiatric profession and the huge pharmaceutical companies which are making billions of dollars a year. Surely it can't be as easy as getting pharmaceutical sales representatives to buy our doctors lunch and explain to them why this new wonder drug is good for their patients with depression and has even fewer side effects than the previous products or versions? Surely, it's not that easy to peddle your billion dollars' worth of drugs to the unsuspecting public? If you want to know a lot more about all of this please visit Robert Whitaker's brilliant site www.madinamerica.com. Better yet, get a copy of his seminal book *Anatomy of an Epidemic,* as well as another book written as far back as 1988 (the very year Prozac was introduced into the market) by Dr. Elliot Valenstein called *Blaming the Brain.*

In *Blaming the Brain,* Dr. Valenstein states the following in his opening chapter: "Throughout this book I will argue that the evidence and arguments supporting all these claims about the relationship of brain chemistry to psychological problems and personality and behavioural traits are far from compelling and are most likely *wrong.* The claim that psychotherapeutic drugs correct a biochemical imbalance that is the root cause of most psychological problems also rests on a *very shaky* scientific foundation. These ideas are simply an unproven hypothesis, but for reasons that will be explored, they are heavily promoted as a well-substantiated explanatory theory. Because these ideas have enormous implications, there is a great need to examine the evidence and basic assumptions much more critically than has been done up to now".[5]

Coming back to 5-HTP, it was banned in America until only recently due to some bad batches that came out of a dodgy manufacturer in Asia, which led to some major government concerns about its properties. I believe that it is now available once more in the USA and is certainly available in Australia through online purchase. However, interestingly enough, you will not find it in any pharmacy or even health food store because it just isn't widely known. And I just have to ask...why?

Why would a naturally occurring supplement (amino acid) that can help to increase serotonin in the least disruptive and invasive way not be on the shelves in pharmacies and heavily promoted by doctors? I will leave you to work that one out.

There are different opinions online about the efficacy of 5-HTP as there are about just about any product or method of healing when it comes to mental health or wellbeing in general. And we are all different. We all respond differently to different products and food substances so there is no one size fits all here of course. But wouldn't you say it's worth trying something *natural* first, with no known side effects or major withdrawal issues, before medically and potentially permanently tampering with our body and brain's neurobiology with so many unknowns?

One caveat here, and this is where the story gets a little thorny. You are not supposed to take 5-HTP if you are already taking an antidepressant (SSRI or SNRI), just in case you end up with a case of serotonin syndrome, which is where your brain/body overpro-

---

[5] Valenstein, Elliot. S. "Blaming the Brain", Free Press (1988).

duces serotonin. This can lead to some potentially harmful outcomes and even (as some sites will say) fatal results. There are very specific signs of potential serotonin syndrome and so if you are starting to experience any of them you would just immediately stop taking the 5-HTP. Research has actually not proven the connection between 5-HTP and serotonin syndrome in humans and suggestions are that it only has potentially harmful outcomes at very high doses.

Just as with any other supplement or medication, you are responsible to monitor how you are reacting to anything you take, whether it's 5-HTP or an aspirin. Just ensure you have the support of a trusted medical doctor but only one who is willing to support what you would like to do with your own body, mind and life.

L-Tyrosine

L-Tyrosine is another amino acid supplement that assists with increasing – through natural means – our levels of dopamine and to some degree norepinephrine. I came across it while searching for natural ways to increase dopamine levels, as I had discovered that serotonin could be increased using 5-HTP, so I wondered whether something similar was the case with dopamine – and sure enough, if you seek you shall find.

L- Tyrosine is one of the amino acids which are the building blocks of protein. The body makes tyrosine from another amino acid called phenylalanine. Tyrosine can also be found in dairy products, meats, fish, eggs, nuts, beans, oats, and wheat. However, trying to get the amount of tyrosine you would need from food has the same issue as trying to get all the Vitamin C you need from oranges or all the Omega 3 Fish Oil you need from eating fish.

Several studies show that tyrosine improves mental performance under stressful conditions, such as military training, cold-induced stress, or noise-induced stress. In addition, tyrosine improves memory under stressful conditions. Taking tyrosine seems to help people who have lost a night's sleep stay alert and some preliminary research suggests that tyrosine improves memory and reasoning in people who are sleep-deprived.[6]

Anecdotal reports from people who have tried L-Tyrosine indicate that it helps increase energy, concentration and mood. Well worth giving it a try, I would say.

St. John's Wort

I am not going to say too much about St. John's Wort, first because I have not really had much experience with it other than to note it is widely prescribed in Germany rather than antidepressants. Apparently, German doctors and the German public in general prefer to use St. John's Wort as a first line treatment for depression and various studies in Germany have shown it to be more effective than a placebo and other anti-depressants. Second, I don't think it is easy to get results from St. John's Wort, as it takes longer to work and it is not clear exactly what dosage one would need to take for it to be considered "effective". I suppose this would be the case with most medicines – whether pharmacological or alternative – when it comes to healing anxiety and depression. Anyone considering using alternative methods for healing anxiety and depression or coming off anti-depressant or anti-anxiety medications needs to be prepared to do their homework and then undertake a bit of experimentation. With regards to St. John's Wort, anyone suffering from mild to moderate depression should probably consider trialing it for themselves but expect it to take a few weeks to a few months to work and to play around with different dosages to see what dosage is right for them. The best thing about St. John's Wort is that there are few to no side-effects and it is a natural herb, therefore it is safe compared to taking any psychiatric drug.

---

[6] http://www.webmd.com/vitamins-supplements/ingredientmono-1037-tyrosine

The B Vitamins

Most people are aware of the need to take a Vitamin B supplement. I remember as a teenager taking a multi-B vitamin supplement during exam times, as I had heard that it was good for stress. I have always equated the taking of a good B vitamin supplement to be synonymous with a good stress management. However, I only found out in the last four years that the B vitamins are also very important in the process of your body converting protein into Tryptophan. Most people are aware that Vitamin B12 is a key vitamin that should be checked if they are suffering with extreme tiredness or having difficulty with their moods. B6 is also important in this process.

Vitamin D

Vitamin D is an essential vitamin known as the sunlight vitamin, since it is synthesized in the skin when exposed to the sun's radiation. It provides benefits for bone structure support, mood state, and much more.

Without adequate levels of vitamin D, many people can suffer from a change in their thinking and mood and there is actually a classification of depression known as SAD (seasonal affective disorder) which can affect many who live in the northern hemisphere, as their exposure to sunlight is limited during the winter months. In these environments, some who do suffer from SAD are encouraged to buy sunlamps and to sit in front of them for about 20 minutes per day. This can often ease depressive symptoms significantly. Another very important action is to ensure adequate levels of vitamin D through supplementation.

The RDA for vitamin D is roughly 400-800 IU, and the optimal level is roughly 2000 IU minimum. The only people who do not need to concern themselves with vitamin D are those who live within the tropics and have frequent sun exposure with bare skin (wearing a t-shirt and shorts is not enough). The recommended daily allowance for Vitamin D is currently set at 400-800IU/day, but this is too low for adults. The safe upper limit in the United States is 2,000IU/day, while in Canada it is 4,000IU/day.

Research suggests that the true safe upper limit is 10,000 IU/day. For moderate supplementation, a 1,000-2,000 IU dose of vitamin D3 is sufficient to meet the needs of most of the population. This is the lowest effective dose range.[7]

Omega 3 fish oil

I had heard about the benefits of taking fish oils in terms of it being good for joints as well as being good for the brain. What I never really knew was that Omega 3 and Omega 6 play pivotal roles in helping the brain function as well as ensuring a healthy environment for your brain cells and neurotransmitters to communicate with each other. Omega 3 fish oils have been proven to reduce depressive symptoms in those experiencing major depressive disorders.[8]

Omega 3 fish oils are also helpful in reducing one of the withdrawal effects of tapering off an anti-depressant, which is the very unpleasant electric "zap"-like sensations that commonly occur when attempting a withdrawal. I still cannot believe how few doctors, psychologists and psychiatrists are aware of this particular withdrawal symptom. In terms of dosage, fish oils come in all shapes and sizes and it was through reading some of information from The Road Back Programme created by James Harper that I understood that not all omega 3 fish oils are created equal. Jim is a pharmacologist who has been helping people reduce or taper off anti-anxiety and anti-depressant medications for over 16 years. Dosage recommendations vary and Jim mentions in his book and

---

[7] https://examine.com/supplements/vitamin-d/
[8] https://examine.com/rubric/effects/view/2/Depression/all/

on his website that the best fish oils are derived from fish such as salmon, herring and trout as opposed to tuna. Effective dose recommendations can range from 400-800mg per day. Ensure that the product is mercury tested and says that it does not have a reflux effect. I wouldn't enjoy smelling like fish breath all day long and I'm sure you don't want to either!

Passionflower

This is another naturally occurring remedy that I found out about from James Harper. James not only researched products that could assist people with drug withdrawal but also sourced and created a range of his own natural products. I did try taking some of James's other products at one stage and there may have been some benefit in taking them but I found the most useful was the Body Cam Formula, which is essentially passionflower mixed with the skin of the Montmort cherry. Jim has created a proprietary product called JNK, which he has trialed in a study in 2016 showing very positive results for both anxiety and depression. For more information, you can visit his site at www.theroadback.org. Passionflower is also available in other commercially available products for relaxation and sleep. I highly recommend a product such as Nature's Own "Sleep Ezy" formula for assistance with sleep; it has passionflower, valerian, hops and chamomile.

Magnesium

Most of us know the sage advice that having a glass of warm milk can assist us with sleep. One of the biggest reasons for this is because milk contains magnesium.

Magnesium is an essential dietary mineral and the second most prevalent electrolyte in the human body. Magnesium deficiencies are common in developed countries. A deficiency increases blood pressure, reduces glucose tolerance and causes neural excitation.

Magnesium deficiencies are common in the Western diet because grains are poor sources of magnesium. Other prominent sources of magnesium, like nuts and leafy vegetables, are not eaten as often. Another reason why you will understand why I now eat the way I do and include a range of leafy vegetables in my diet on a very regular basis.

You can also use a magnesium supplemented which has the ability to improve a deficiency, act as a sedative, reduce blood pressure and even improve insulin sensitivity. Maintaining healthy magnesium levels is also associated with a protective effect against depression and ADHD. The standard dose for magnesium supplementation is 200-400mg per day. It is best taken in the evening, as it helps to relax the muscles and assists with sleep. When looking at the diets of persons suffering from depression, there appears to be an inverse relationship between dietary magnesium intake and depressive symptoms.[9]

Zinc

Zinc is one of the 24 micronutrients needed for survival. It is found in meat, egg, and legume products. Oysters are particularly good sources of zinc. It is very important for the functioning of the enzyme, hormone, and immune systems.[10] Zinc has two standard dosages. The low dosage is 5-10mg, while the high dosage is 25-45mg. The low dose works well as a daily preventative, while the high dosage should be taken by anyone at risk for a zinc deficiency. Secondary to an improvement in overall mood, aggressive symptoms have been noted to be reduced with low dose zinc supplementation.

These then are some of the more natural approaches to nutrition and supplementation when it comes to helping reduce anxious or

---

[9] https://examine.com/supplements/magnesium/
[10] https://examine.com/supplements/zinc/

depressive symptoms rather than going head first (excuse the pun) into dangerous psychiatric drugs.

The regime that I eventually adopted with regards to my diet may be considered by some to be quite extreme but today I live anxiety, depression and antidepressant free. I do not eat meat or chicken. My dinners are mostly made of a combination of fish, rice, and vegetables. Many nights I will just eat a vegetable soup containing cabbage, onion, garlic and celery with gluten free bread.

I drink at least eight cups of hot water every single day and most days I don't eat breakfast. I usually have my morning coffee (flat white with soy or almond milk) and I may have a snack of fruit or gluten free toast around mid-morning, but that's it until lunch time.

Lunch is usually rice and vegetables or some smoked salmon on toasted gluten free bread with humus.

I don't expect anyone to do what I do with regards to my diet and exercise regime. However, it is what I believe helped me to completely turn my life around and to finally break free from psychiatric medications and find my true self again.

I am infinitely happier, healthier and more productive and connected to life than I have ever been.

If my way of life can inspire others to make shifts or changes to their own diet and lifestyle and this leads them to a greater quality of life then I can only be delighted.

If even one of the tips above helps you lessen your anxiety or depression then it was probably worth the price you paid for the whole book.

In the next chapter we are going to talk about probably one of the most critical elements of overcoming anxiety and depression known to man and that is cardiovascular exercise, so get ready to...run for your life!

CHAPTER SIX –

Run for your life

"You must do the thing you think you cannot do."

— Eleanor Roosevelt

Exercise has a powerful antidepressant effect. It has been proven that people are far less likely to relapse after recovering from depression if they exercise three times a week or more. Exercise makes serotonin more available for binding to receptor sites on nerve cells, so it can compensate for changes in serotonin levels as you taper off SSRIs and other medications that target the serotonin system.[11]

One of the absolutely irrefutable natural techniques or approaches to overcoming anxiety and depression, as well as antidepressants, is regular and fairly rigorous cardiovascular exercise.

Everyone is different, of course, in what kind of exercise they like to do. Some people like to walk, some like to do yoga, some like to play soccer or push weights in the gym.

However, I need to make one thing absolutely clear here.

---

[11] http://www.health.harvard.edu/diseases-and-conditions/going-off-antidepressants

You will never get the kinds of benefits and mental health results you want to get by doing any of these things. And there are very real and scientific reasons for this relating to the chemistry of your body and how that impacts your thinking, emotions, mental health and overall wellbeing.

As I have already discussed, one of the key contributors to increased anxiety and depression is potential lowered levels of serotonin in your body and brain. Now, again, this has never been CONCLUSIVELY proven. And whilst what I am suggesting here to you about cardiovascular exercise is meant to be connected to helping to elevate your serotonin levels, the body and brain are much too complex for that to be the only factor or reason that you are going to feel so much better.

Serotonin itself is one of the most widely spread neurotransmitters in your body and it plays a major role in a whole range of critical functions, including motivation, sleep, sex drive, energy, appetite and general physiological functioning of your entire system.

So too, cardiovascular activity that involves the following is the most likely to have the greatest impact on your mental and physical wellbeing:

1. It must be for at least 20-30 minutes
2. Your heart rate must be increased and held at the increased rate for the majority of the time you are exercising
3. You have to be sweating – preferably a lot!

Doing yoga is fine and many people absolutely swear by it and I fully believe it is one of the few "non-cardio" activities that can be very beneficial for your mental health.

I believe it is so effective because it is a combination of meditation through breath, body work and mindfulness, which brings you into the present moment. It also provides social connection because most people do it in a class setting. It can also be quite strenuous from what I understand, which is great as it is then able to provide some of the benefits I have been describing that you need in order to elevate your serotonin levels.

I have never done yoga even though I am sure I will be joining all the yogi bears soon because I fully get the benefits and I am actually very keen to do it.

What I absolutely *know*, however, is that when it comes to mental health and those who struggle with anxiety and in particular with depression, THERE IS NO SUBSTITUTE for rigorous cardiovascular exercise when it comes to physical activity.

For me, and for so many of my clients as well as others I have researched, the activity that seems to work the best is running.

When I suggest to people who are struggling with stress, anxiety and depression that they should start jogging or running, I am often met with resistance. The excuses are usually along the lines of:

"I don't have the time"
"I can't get to the gym"
"I don't like sweating"
"I can't get up that early" (that was my excuse too)
"I'm not a runner"
"I have children" (so do I, three of them)
"I prefer going for a walk – that is the same thing, right?"
"I'm a single parent" (So am I)
"My work is too demanding"
"I don't like running"
"I used to be a runner but I can't fit it in anymore"

The list of excuses goes on and I am sure you could add some of your own personal ones to it as well, right? All nonsense. None of those excuses hold up to the light of truth and what you are truly capable of doing in this life. And please don't get me wrong. There is no judgement here. I have had and still do have plenty of my own reasons and excuses for not doing some of the things I know I need to do to. But, for the most part, I just don't allow myself to hook into these anymore because I have proven to myself that excuses are just excuses and beliefs are just beliefs and you can choose something else. Especially when you get clear on why you want to and need to change. Maybe you need to hit rock bottom like I did before you realise it's game time and you're playing for the highest stakes you've ever played for in your life.

If you identify with any of the above excuses, IT'S OK! We are going to get you past all that nonsense. You've come to the right place! I understand the traps that hold you back because I used plenty of them myself. But no more.

However, you have to at least be willing to see that the thoughts and beliefs you have about why you can't jog or run are just mental traps that your mind is playing on you to try to keep you in the negative and depressed state you're in. It's one of the traps of anxiety and depression, remember? So let's see if we can bring in some very important reasons and knowledge and some major motivation for you to understand why you need to do a cardiovascular activity like running, cross trainer, cycling, treadmill or any other kind of exercise that gets the blood pumping, oxygen flowing and sweat dripping.

Here we go...

A regular cardiovascular activity, let's say a minimum of three times a week and ideally five to six days a week, has been PROVEN to relieve symptoms of stress, anxiety and depression. Through study after study as well as through meta studies (which means studies that look at hundreds of other research study data as a whole), we see that it practically never fails to help elevate mood, increase clarity of thought and increase energy levels.

Dr. Gary Small, writing for Psychology Today, refers to a study completed by Duke University which compared the antidepressant effects of aerobic exercise training to a popular antidepressant medication, as well as a placebo sugar pill. They randomized depressed patients to one of the three groups and found that after four months about 40 percent of the subjects in total were no longer depressed.

Now here is the fascinating finding which is almost glossed over in Dr. Small's article: Those who exercised or received the medicine had higher and comparable response rates, but they were only slightly better than the placebo group. Those who exercised at a moderate level - about 40 minutes three to five days each week - experienced the greatest antidepressant effect. So they interpreted that to mean that exercise was just as good as medicine. How this can be so totally glossed over is simply beyond me! They basically found, as they so often do in these studies, that exercise or in other studies CBT (cognitive behavioural therapy), was *as effective* as antidepressants but fail to mention the absolute horrors people go through when going onto, staying on or trying to come off the drugs. No such thing happens with a moderate exercise regime or CBT. In fact, as the subjects have now learned new habits and skills to cope with stress, anxiety and depression they feel more confident and competent to deal with what life throws at them. And so, their chance of relapse is lowered.

Doing moderate cardiovascular exercise helps to kick-start people into being able to resolve whatever life events and issues they may be struggling with. Through personal examples of nearly everyone who has ever conquered anxiety or depression, we find a strikingly similar pattern emerge of people finding their way back from anxiety and depression through fairly intense cardiovascular exercise.

How does this kind of cardiovascular exercise routine help?

I believe there are a range of reasons; some are purely physiological in nature and some are psychological and even spiritual.

First, physiologically speaking, we all know that the immediate effect of going for that jog, run, ride, etc. is that we get an increase in endorphins. Endorphins are natural peptide chemical messengers – much like serotonin and dopamine, which are produced in your body and interact with receptors in your brain to help you feel focused, less impacted by pain and put you in a better mood. In fact, endorphins have a lot in common with opiate-based painkillers. However, they are obviously good for you and there are no nasty side effects.

When we run, we also get the blood pumping through our veins, arteries, organs and brains. Put simply, we need our blood to circulate throughout the body and brain in order to survive and function properly. We need the blood to carry oxygen to all parts of the body, and the brain in particular thrives on oxygen. Now, imagine what spending endless hours indoors, not moving much and not breathing deeply actually does to your physiology and your mentality.

This is why I recommend doing your activity *outdoors*, where you can breathe in and massively increase the amount of oxygen in your bloodstream. Remember, without oxygen you would DIE. There are many things in life that you can do without and you wouldn't die...oxygen isn't one of them. However, what most people don't seem to realise is that there is also a quality and quantity effect when it comes to oxygen.

It's not just about getting in "any old oxygen". We need good quality oxygen every single day in order to live the healthiest and happiest lives that we can.

So, I would like you to reflect on this question: Why is it that every single technique that helps us to feel better in life BEGINS with BREATHING more effectively?

It doesn't matter if we are talking about meditating, yoga, mindfulness, exercising or just going about our day-to-day lives.

Why is it that when we are stressed or anxious, we find that we are breathing in a very shallow way? Because this is one of the first things that happens automatically when we begin to feel tension or stress in life.

And this is why one of the first techniques I teach people who come to me for counselling is how to breathe properly and realise that whilst breathing is an automatic function of the body, it is also a function that we can CHOOSE to take full control of when we are feeling stressed, anxious or depressed. We can engage consciously with our breathing and alter it in a manner of seconds. And within minutes, between three to five minutes, we completely alter what is happening in our bodies and minds.

As an example, I had a young woman come to see me recently who was suffering with some severe anxiety and was also beginning to experience symptoms of having panic attacks, although she didn't really know it until we spoke. She told me how she struggled to get any sleep at night because her mind would race so fast. No matter how tired she was, once she tried to fall asleep her mind would race. She was starting to experience symptoms of panic in public places as well, particularly if she was alone and perceived that people were observing and possibly judging her. She would then begin to experience "black patches around her field of vision," she said to me. She also mentioned feeling hot and flushed and her chest would tighten and she would feel out of breath and sometimes dizzy, as if she was about to faint. These are classical anxiety and panic symptoms.

Towards the end of our first session together, after observing how she began to display the signs of high anxiety during the sessions as she spoke about some of the situations that made her anxious, I told her that we were going to practice breathing. I had already normalised her experiences and explained they were very common, and I also explained what was happening in her body with the mix of oxygen to carbon dioxide that was leading to the symptoms. She was intrigued to say the least and I could see the relief on her face as she realised the relatively simple explanation for what was happening to her.

I then got her to show me how she took a deep breath, as I do with all my clients. Sure enough, she took a deep breath to the top section of her lungs, lifted her shoulders up and then looked at me. I smiled at her and said, "That's actually a shallow breath, not a deep breath."

I explained the technique that I teach all my clients that has been proven to work very effectively, which is to breath in slowly for a four-second count through the nose and then four seconds out through the mouth, making a sound as the air escapes and paying attention to the sound as a little bit of a distraction. I also got her to focus on a point in the room. Within two minutes, I could see her beginning to settle and as we got to the third minute, she actually yawned. This is always a great sign that the brain has received the message that it is not under threat and that it can calm down.

This short anecdote, which is just one of hundreds of clients I have taught, shows just how simple some of these remedies can be when it comes to overcoming anxiety.

It is also a very simple and effective example of how correct breathing is critical to our mental and physical health.

Thank goodness that we do have control over this critical element of our wellbeing because it is a very powerful tool that we ALL have to help us settle our emotions down, release the tension in our bodies and begin to feel more peaceful, focused and motivated again.

As soon as we start to move our bodies through exercise we alter the way we are breathing and begin to bring much greater quantities of oxygen into our body and brain, and this is essential in helping to change our mental and emotional state.

Why does the activity need to be fairly intense?

The reason I keep saying "fairly" intense exercise is because there is some thinking and experience out there by a percentage of those who have struggled with anxiety and depression that too much exercise of this sort can be counterproductive to getting better. I don't disagree with them about this because I have experienced this to some extent when I was struggling with the antidepressants and tried to use intense running to relieve the incredible amount of anxiety I was experiencing. On one particular business trip, where I was meant to be providing senior management coaching for a customer of mine, I was struggling with some major anxiety and I tried to run my way out of it. And it didn't work at all. It took too much energy out of me and then I just felt depleted and overwhelmed. However, I certainly wasn't eating the way I am today or running as consistently.

One particular reader of one of my articles wrote a comment online saying that I was wrong and that her husband had to completely cut back on his exercise when he was going through the struggle of withdrawing from antidepressant medications. I can appreciate that and I will *always* say that *you* are the only one who knows what you are thinking and feeling on any given day and how you respond to any particular food, drink, activity, exercise, conversation, drug or therapy, etc. This is very much the core of my message in this book to all of you anyway. You need to get in the driving seat and take control of your own life experience.

Further to that point, although I will be sharing with you what MY regimen is when it comes to exercise and what worked FOR ME to help get me over the last hurdle of setting myself free from the antidepressant drugs after 17 years of being trapped, it may not be the same for you. I would never dream of prescribing when or how your recovery will happen. I can only attempt to highlight for you what has been proven to work for the majority of people through research and then beyond the research and science, I will share with you a few things that may seem a little "out there" about how to turn your life around. These are ideas, concepts and practices that I have discovered through my ceaseless search for what works to overcome anxiety and depression as well as how to live the best lives that we possibly can.

However, it will forever remain your CHOICE, whether you decide to try some of things I recommend here but you may not have the same results. It's not a recipe, it's just a guideline...just a map, not the territory.

Let me give you a little more about my own story with exercise and martial arts.

I was never much of an athlete during high school. I never did any exercise-related hobbies although I had tried judo and Kung Fu for very short periods of time as a teenager. I also took tennis lessons at one stage but most of my activities were with friends, either playing tennis or cricket. Exercise was never something that my parents encouraged or pushed for, right or wrong.

However, just after I finished high school in 1994, I started Tae Kwon Do and as part of our training every Saturday afternoon we would go for a 4km run. I never liked the idea of jogging or running that much, and the first time I did that 4km run, barefoot in 34 degree heat and on the pavement, I ended up with blisters the size of lemons on the soles of my feet and couldn't walk very well for the next week or so. However, over the weeks and months and years that followed, I began to enjoy jogging. However, I never jogged more than once a week, which tended to be before our Saturday afternoon Tae Kwon Do classes. And that was *before* the punishing class began!

When I stopped doing Tae Kwon Do around the year 2000, I also stopped running. However, in 2011, when my marriage ended and I was struggling to get used to not seeing my boys as much, who were then five and two and a half years old, I knew I had to start to exercise quite rigorously again. I was going through one of the most difficult times of my life. I was going through hell and the antidepressant I was taking at the time wasn't working; in fact, it was making everything much worse, I just didn't know it at the time. I thought, as most people do, that my life situation was the primary cause of the unbelievable amount of anxiety and depression that I was experiencing and that the antidepressants were helping or at least keeping me afloat. It's one thing to struggle with a traumatic life event and suffer the mental and emotional pain that comes with that; it's another thing altogether to get through that with drugs completely screwing your brain and body around as well. And then I had psychiatrists playing God with my life by suggesting I increase my dose or switch to some other – sometimes much worse – drug. It would be not long after this that I seriously began to question what was happening with me, particularly in regards to the unbelievable amount of anxiety I was experiencing on a daily basis.

As I said, I knew I needed to get myself back to cardiovascular activity. In fact, I will never forget a friend of mine mentioning to me that he too had suffered with depression – something I had not known at the time as we were not that close; however, I doubt even his closest friends knew – and he said the one thing that really helped him recover was running rigorously and consistently.

My cousin had taken up cycling and so I decided to give that a try. However, I found it didn't give me the kind of result I was looking for and I didn't particularly enjoy cycling.

It was then that I really began to jog at least two to three times per week. The mental benefits were there for sure and I became quite consistent in my running up until 2013, when I managed to get off the antidepressants for the first time in over 13 years. That victory back in July 2013 was to be short-lived, however. If you would like to read a bit about the lead up to that story, as I do not have the space to describe it all here, please head over to Robert

Whitaker's brilliant website, www.madinamerica.com, and search for my story. You will find part one, part two and part three in which I detail my difficult journey with the antidepressants right through to finally breaking free from them after seventeen years and reclaiming my life.

And so, in August 2013, the "relationship" I had with my daughter's mother ended. This happened at the same time as I changed careers back into the field of human resources and suffered an existential crisis and the terrible feeling that things were going in the complete wrong direction. The move to the new organisation ended up being a complete disaster for me and I ended up leaving after becoming horribly anxious and depressed. Over the next few years I did run fairly consistently and this did certainly help me cope with all the pressure I was under, both financially and emotionally.

There are many things I did between 2015 and 2017, which included changing my work life, diet, living situation, financial situation and which seemed to include a number of seemingly coincidental events – but I now know that they were synchronistic, not random events. However, it was only at the beginning of 2018 that I began to get up every single morning at 5am and run. At the time I began this, I had done hardly *any* exercise in the previous two years, partly due to what that one reader had said about exercise sometimes making things worse for those trying to taper off antidepressants. However, that was a *huge* mistake and created a false belief in me which I have now obliterated. It was the running, the change in mentality that came with it, as well as the significant changes to my diet that led to me getting completely off the drugs in the space of two months. Something that, by all accounts, should not have been possible...especially for someone who had been on them for so long.

Getting up early was inspired by a reconnection with my Tae Kwon Do master but it was also inspired by a sixty-year-old client of mine whose two brothers had both died due to depression. One became terribly ill on antidepressants and the other suicided by hanging himself.

My client suffered with depression himself but had never resorted to taking any medications after seeing what it had done to his older brother, who he lost to suicide in his thirties. Even after almost thirty years, his eyes would well up with tears when he would talk to me about his brother and he would take out a wallet-sized black and white photo of his brother to show me every now and then.

This man and I developed a strong bond and rapport during our counselling sessions together. He would sit there, shake his head and ask me why it had to be this way. Why he had to lose his brothers in this way to depression. We both just had to sit with it together and accept that sometimes there are no real answers to what happens to some people in life, but we can do everything we can do to help those who can still be helped, before it's too late.

The reason I share this particular client's story with you is because he became an inspiration to me because of the way he would keep his own depression at bay by going down to the ocean, EVERY SINGLE morning, and swimming for about thirty minutes. Summer, winter, rain or hail, he would be down at the ocean pool around 5:30am for his swim. His colleagues at work used to joke with him – being part of a very blokey workplace – that he was crazy. But in fact, he was the sanest person I have ever met and he knew what needed to be done to keep his spirits up and for him to keep moving forward with joy in his own life, even after suffering the tragedy of losing both of his brothers to depression.

I realised at some point that a big part of the solution for most of us who struggle with anxiety or depression is to exercise every single day...or as close to it as we can. As you saw from the Duke University research study, the people who experienced the greatest relief from their depression exercised moderately for about 40 minutes four to five times a week. My experience has been the same. And indeed, that is what I started to do and is what I still do six days a week.

During the week it's usually a 4-5 km run and on the weekend I do at least one 10-12km run...something I would never even have dreamed I could do. It is truly amazing what you can do when you really DECIDE that you are no longer willing to put up with anxiety and depression and all the damage, pain and heartache they are causing you. It is a very small price to pay, getting up every morning - rain or shine - and running for my life. My life is worth it and so is your

CHAPTER SEVEN

Meditation is Mandatory

"The goal of meditation is not to control your thoughts but to stop letting them control you"

- Unknown

I wasn't going to include a chapter on meditation in this book because I have actually written about it in my first book. However, as I reflected further about just exactly what helped me the most during some of the most difficult and dark times that I have experienced in my life with anxiety, depression and antidepressant withdrawal; meditation stood out as a tool that is absolutely essential.

This is why I titled this chapter *meditation is mandatory* because I think a lot of people don't really understand just how integral meditation is to a well-balanced, calm, focused and productive life. When it comes to mental health difficulties, there really is no substitute for it. A close second might be yoga, however, as you will see, meditation is a tool that is going to be there in the moments when you need it the most.

When I ask clients in counselling who are struggling with stress, anxiety or depression whether they meditate I get quite a mixed response. Some may have thought of doing it and tried it once or twice and simply given up. Others may have used it consistently at times but it is quite rare to find someone who says "Oh yes, of course I meditate...every single day!"

What I invariably hear when I talk to people about meditation is something like:

"I can't meditate"
"Meditation is airy fairy"
"It's a waste of time"
"My mind is too busy"
"It doesn't work for me" ... and my favourite
"I don't have time".

Let us get the "I don't have time" thing out of the way right from the start of this chapter.

And I will make it plain for you...you can't *afford to not have time* for meditation.

Not if you are serious about creating a better life for yourself and the people you love.

I specifically included the people you love because when you learn how to meditate (and believe me the process is simple) – you become a better version of yourself for those around you. You become a calmer, happier and more focused parent, partner, colleague, or leader.

In Buddhism, meditation is described as a rigorous process of mental training in which the mind observes itself. As human beings, this is one of the core differences between us and the animals i.e. our ability to become aware of thinking itself. If we so choose, we can become acutely aware of what is happening within us and therefore the precursors or drivers of our behaviour. Of course, not everyone uses their awareness and the majority of people will react just the same as an animal does to a trigger or stimulus in their environment. However, that does not mean they don't have choice to stop in the moment before reacting, reflect and then respond with purposeful, thoughtful and controlled behaviour. Some people *choose* not to see that they have this capability.

When we begin to meditate and settle our minds, we are able to develop what is referred to as *attentional stability*[12] – which means we are able to train our minds to focus in on *nothingness* and bring ourselves to the present moment. Through this we are able to develop our *attentional clarity* – which means we are able to have a much greater level of awareness with regards to the thoughts, sensations and emotions that we are experiencing at that particular point in time. We then gain a greater sense of what is happening inside of us and through settling and calming everything down we are able to hit the *reset button* and then choose – much more consciously and deliberately – the thoughts, emotions and behaviours that are more useful and positive for us and the people around us.

Some of the benefits we achieve through meditation are:

- A calmer emotional state
- A more relaxed body
- A quieter and clearer mind
- A sense of inner peace
- Greater levels of focus and motivation
- A renewing of energy through dissipating negative and destructive moods
- An understanding of the difference in our experience of frantic, negative and often overwhelming thoughts and calm, positive and motivating thoughts.

---

[12] Begley, Sharon. *Train your Mind, Change your Brain.* 2007. Ballantine Books

When it comes to tools which we have at our disposal that do not involve trying to think our way out of anxiety and depression; cardiovascular exercise and meditation are two of the most important tools you *must* have in your arsenal. As I have said before, when you are stuck in a mental fog of negativity, emotional turmoil and pain, your odds of thinking your way out of that mess are very low. When that avenue is closed, you will need to use tools which involve changing your physiology first before you can begin to take back control of your thinking and steer yourself in a more desirable direction.

When some people hear the word *meditation*, it conjures up images of a monk sitting in his orange robe under a tree high somewhere up on a mountain. They might think that it's all too "airy fairy' and that sitting down to breathe in a funny way is not a very practical or scientific way to help them lower their stress levels, cope with anxiety or relieve depression.

I am going to assume you are open to using meditation because you probably wouldn't have bought this book in the first place and you definitely wouldn't have gotten this far into the book if you weren't ready to give something like the natural and proven technique of meditation a go.

I hope I have now got your attention and done a good sales job so far for meditation, yes? However, let me take it a step further and hit you with some hard facts and neuroscience for those of you who may still be a little sceptical about the benefits of meditation.

Sharon Begley is a Newsweek and Boston Globe health sciences writer and has won many awards for her research and journalism. In 2007, Sharon published the book *Train your Mind, Change your Brain* in which she reports on a large scale study which involved Harvard neuroscientists and Tibetan monks. The Dalai Lama has always been fascinated by the relationship between eastern philosophy and practice and how it relates to and can be connected to scientific inquiry. In this unbelievably ambitious study, the researchers had to get Buddhist monks who basically live their lives in isolation and who have less than zero interest in the outside world or advancing medical science, to agree to undertake MRI brain scans whilst in various meditative states.

The researchers managed to finally get a few of the monks to agree to travel to the USA to be assessed.

What they found after running various tests was that the monks had the ability to change their brain chemistry at a level that was completely unexpected as they entered various states of meditation. They also had the capacity to engage with various emotions – specifically compassion – at will.

Begley's research and book contributed to the growing body of evidence around the neuroplasticity of the brain and how the brain can indeed generate new neurons as well as neural pathways as opposed to our previous belief that this was not possible and that the brain's functioning was pretty much set in stone.

What this means for you, enthusiastic meditator, is that you have a simple, free and non-toxic tool at your disposal which has the capacity to not only help you feel calmer at any time you decide to use it but it also has the capacity over time to help you shift your brain's structure and how it reacts to various life events.

Meditation has the ability to literally help you rewire your brain and develop new neural pathways which is what we most need to do in order to overcome anxiety and depression.

Learning and practicing the skill of meditation is even more critical for those who are trying to taper off antidepressants.

Let me give you give you an example from my own life of how meditation has helped me when it comes to overcoming stress, anxiety, fatigue and being, at times, very overwhelmed.

During the period when I was working as a contract counsellor and I was seeing approximately thirty people a week for counselling, I was also struggling with anxiety, depression, antidepressant withdrawal at various times, divorce, and ongoing financial stress.

There were days when I just didn't know how I was going to get through or how on earth I was going to find the clarity and the energy I needed to be of service to the people who were coming to see me. Firstly, let me just say that I pride myself on my counselling skills and my ability to help people through their struggles and most trying times in life and that my results speak for themselves.

People always coming back and utilise all the sessions that they are entitled to and would often want to continue to see me beyond the sessions they got through their employers or through the government Medicare rebates. I have been consistently rated at the highest levels across every measure used to assess the experience of clients who come to see me. I would not have been able to achieve this if I wasn't delivering for people and helping them improve their lives in a measurable way.

Having said that, during those days back in 2014-2015, I felt like I was drowning. And I can tell you, hands down, that meditation was an absolute life saver for me during that time.

I would often use small gaps between my counselling appointments to do mini-meditations. Sometimes they were only ten minutes in length but they always had some impact. They always gave me some level of relief from the anxiety or the fatigue that I was struggling with. When I was able to quiet my mind and body and continue with a fifteen to twenty-minute meditation, I would usually get the best results. I would come out of those mini sessions with a renewed sense of peace and wellbeing. Everything would settle and I would find my mind calmer, clearer and I would usually feel a rising of my energy levels as well. As I developed my practice further, and as I still use it today, I have been able to engage with a breathing-meditative practice which now allows me to rejuvenate myself and feel as if I have just woken from a few hours of high-quality sleep. I am sometimes quite astounded at how something so simple and so quickly employed, can have lasting effects for the rest of my day.

Through practicing the very simple meditative practice that I will share with you here and which I have taught to hundreds of my clients, you too will have the capability to grab fifteen minutes out of your day and reset your mental and physical energy. Find a time and place to do this midday is highly recommended as this allows you to release any built up negative emotions and to release any tension that may have been building in your body during the course of your morning. Of course, it is completely up to you when you practice the meditation but I would suggest you try to at least do it once a day.

As I often say to my clients: *there are no bad meditations*. At worst, you will have given yourself a much-needed time out and you will have experienced at least some improvement in how you are feeling and at best; you will experience a complete recovery, renewed energy, greater mental clarity and a massive boost to your level of mental and physical wellbeing.

You may not be able to meditate somewhere quiet during your working day and that is just fine, but you can certainly find fifteen minutes to do it when you wake up or before you go to sleep at night. Practicing meditation before bed is an ideal way to help your mind and body prepare for a better night's sleep.

There is nothing mystical about the three-step process I am about to share with you – even though it can certainly lead to much greater awareness and a feeling of being connected to everything around you. When I explain it to my clients, I make the case very simply and clearly:

The goal of meditation – for you – is to reduce the number of thoughts that are coming at you and to lower the overall level of "activation" you may be experiencing in your mind and body which you may not even realise is happening. When we are stressed, anxious or depressed there is just too much going on in our minds and bodies which leads to an underlying sense of agitation, foreboding and discomfort. If we ignore it, it only gathers momentum and gets worse.

Through this simple process of meditation, we bring our awareness to what is happening in our mind and body as we use our breathing and physiology to settle our entire system down. We then proceed to use our conscious awareness of our own thinking to let go of thought until we reach a very special state of being which can only be experienced. Words don't teach, but they may instruct you into your own experience and that is where the magic happens. So, go for it. Test this out and don't give up just because your mind doesn't want to cooperate in the beginning.

A simple three-step process to peace and wellbeing

Firstly, there are some initial *ground rules* when it comes to practicing this technique which you should follow:

Begin by ensuring that you will have *no distractions* for the next fifteen to twenty minutes. If that means switching your phone to silent, finding a quiet office space, telling your kids to not disturb you unless the house is on fire, telling your husband/wife/partner/flatmate that you are not to be disturbed under threat of legal action...do it. Whatever you need to do to ensure you will not be interrupted.

Find a comfortable spot, it can be on a chair, a couch, bed, floor...it doesn't really matter but there is one thing that you have to do which is to sit comfortably with your back straight up and head up. Support your lower back with a cushion if you need. I like getting myself into a meditative pose which involves sitting up straight, legs crossed in front of me and hands resting gently on my legs or knees. The reason you want to ensure you are upright is because your brain is very clever and it actually knows the difference between when you are lying down or sitting upright. We have something inside our brains called the *reticular activating system* which is able to identify when we are lying down or sitting up and which will signal the brain whether that is might be time to fall asleep.

Two points on mediation and sleeping. If you are using meditation to help you fall asleep that is fine and well but it is not the purpose of this exercise. However, you must understand here that you absolutely WILL NOT get the kinds of benefits that you need to get from this meditation if you fall asleep before you get yourself to the end of fifteen to twenty minutes.

Loosen any restrictive clothing like belts and ties to ensure and unrestricted flow or breathing, movement and energy in your body.

And now begin with your breathing...

Start to take in breath through your nose and use a four second count breathing in and pushing the air down to your stomach-diaphragm. You can even place your hand on your stomach and feel it expand life a balloon. You should ensure that when you breathe in deeply your shoulders and upper part of your chest remain still. Many people make the mistake of thinking that taking a deep breath involved bringing in more air to the top part of their chest-lungs. However, this is actually a *shallow* breath.

Now, breathe out through your mouth and listen to the sound of your breath escaping. Count the four seconds out as well as this provides the added benefit of creating a mini distraction for your brain and assists with the settling down of the thoughts.

Continue to breath in through your nose and out through your mouth counting four seconds in and four seconds out. Do this in a rhythmic manner without necessarily holding onto the breath. There are many breathing techniques out there and some suggest holding the breath however the kind of breathing and meditation I am suggesting here requires that you create a rhythmic cycle of oxygen coming in and carbon dioxide going out in even proportions. The reason for this is that it helps to send the right signal to your brain that *everything is okay* and that your brain can begin to let go and settle.

You should carry on doing this for the first three to five minutes of your meditation. That's step one.

Step two is to now begin to focus on your body. As you continue to breathe in the rhythmic manner above you now begin to do what is called a *body scan*. Here you start at the top of your head and just become aware and notice any tension that you are holding in your body. If you do notice any tension, mentally instruct your body to let go of it. You may find yourself moving a certain muscle or body part. In my own practice I will find that as I get close to the three-minute mark of breathing I naturally start to move my jaw as I tend to hold a lot of tension there without even realising it. It is different for everyone and people hold tension in different places in the body. You may, for instance, notice as you begin to relax that your chest is quite tight. Use the breath coming in to imagine sending the breath to that part of your body and pushing or easing the tension away.

Continue the body scan and the letting go of any tension in your body for the next three to five minutes.

You are now approximately eight to ten minutes into your meditation and you should now be starting to feel significantly different to how you felt when you first began.

The final step is to return your breathing to normal and to now become aware of any thoughts that may be floating around in your mind. Here we use a concept from the psychological discipline called acceptance and commitment therapy (ACT) which is to become aware of the thoughts but not engage with them. This is certainly harder than it seems and is probably one of the main reasons some people don't think meditation works. I suggest to my clients that they imagine this part of the process as a ping pong match between themselves and their brains. The brain will send a raft of thoughts at you and your job is just to acknowledge the thought and then mentally knock it straight back and out of sight. The same thought may come straight back at you and you just notice it and knock it away again.

The next thought will come and you just notice it and try your best not to follow where it wants to lead you. Another analogy I like to use is that your untrained brain is just like a puppy running around in an open field or park. It sniffs at something and it's off like a bolt of lightning – chasing whatever it is that caught its attention. Your job is to be firm and to bring it back, acknowledge the thought that it "found" so fascinating, and get it to *sit*. Anyone who has ever had a puppy and tried to train it to sit down and be still will know it takes time and patience. It is very much the same with your brain. You have not engaged with your mind in this way before and even if you have, that doesn't mean your mind isn't going to try go off on a tangent for a few seconds or minutes when you try to settle and meditate.

Know this: it is natural! That is what the brain does and its okay. But you don't have to allow it to keeping run amok when you are deliberate in your meditation. You just need to keep persisting in bringing your attention and focus back to the front of your mind. You may want to use imagery to help you. Some people like to use the image of your mind space being like the sky and every thought like a cloud that passes by. You just notice the cloud-thoughts drifting across the screen of your mind and then watch them float out of your range of vision. Let them go and keep letting them go until....

Things begin to get quieter. Less thoughts are being generated for your attention because what begins to happen is that your brain realises that you are *not paying attention* to its rants and that you are not willing to engage with any particular thought and so, it gives up, temporarily, sending you all those thoughts.

This is the sweet spot. This is the place you want to be heading into as you get closer to the end of your fifteen minutes and, believe me, when you do get there you will want to hold that space for another few minutes. Generally speaking, you really don't need to go longer than twenty minutes so aim for that as a maximum but feel free to go longer if you want.

What you will find as you enter this state of relaxed breathing, relaxed physiology and relaxed and peaceful thinking without thought is that you will experience the unusual state of being called serenity. It is here – in this state of peace and calm – that you are able to reconnect to the core of your being. It is here that you are able to access a connection to another part of yourself that exists behind the veil of active thought. It is here that you will find your wellbeing, your truth and your freedom from stress, anxiety, worry, fatigue and depression.

I encourage you to give this a try if you have never tried it before and I sincerely wish for you that you get to that place that I have just described of no thought and no emotion because it is here that you will discover that you have within you the capability to give yourself relief from anxiety and depression at just about any time you choose.

It is not infallible this process. There will be times when you may be too distressed to even try to engage in meditation and that may be when you need to use other tools such as cardiovascular activity or you may need to reach out and speak to someone but make no mistake: when it comes to overcoming anxiety and depression and leaving antidepressants behind forever, meditation is mandatory

CHAPTER EIGHT

Science versus Spirit

"We need to put spirit back into the equation when we want to improve our physical and our mental health. We are not powerless biochemical machines... and so popping a pill every time we are mentally or physically out of tune is not the answer. It is not gene-directed hormones and neurotransmitters that control our bodies and our minds but our beliefs which control our bodies, our minds, and thus our lives"

Dr Bruce Lipton, PhD - *Internationally recognised cell biologist, lecturer and author*

Wayne Dyer used to say if you asked any scientist fifty years ago if they believed in God most of them would say, "Of course not, I'm a scientist!" but ask most scientists today if they believe in God and most would say, "Of course I do, I'm a scientist!"

So whereas before science focused and reported only what could be proven through observation and analysis, scientists today are realising that there are things they have discovered through the deep study of reality which just aren't explainable. Some of the greatest scientific minds of our generation have, after spending their entire lives in the scientific field, come to the conclusion that there are mysteries to the human mind, body and spirit that we have not been able to explain through scientific methods.

In *The Biology of Belief*, Dr. Bruce Lipton discusses how he had to leave the university he was teaching at after coming to the conclusion that what he had been teaching for years was wrong.

After delving deeply into the human genome and genetic coding, his research and rediscovery of quantum physics began to show that our genetics played a much smaller part in what happened to us over time than was originally suspected. Dr. Lipton discovered through his in-depth research into matter itself that there is no sufficient linear "Newtonian" explanation for the way particles behave. He discovered that although biologists and scientists to this day believe in the pure cause and effect hypothesis of health and disease, they are missing a vital part of the puzzle, which is that energy itself is the driving force behind the creation of particles in the universe. This was spelled out in Einstein's' famous formula $e=mc^2$ (energy = matter (mass) multiplied by the speed of light squared).

Einstein revealed that we do not live in a universe with discrete, physical objects separated by dead space. The Universe is one indivisible, dynamic whole in which energy and matter are so deeply entangled it is impossible to consider them as independent elements.

The field of epi-genetics is now beginning to show that it is the ***expression*** of our genes or what triggers their expression that is infinitely more important to what happens to us than our actual genetics. What this points to is that our biology is not – as was thought previously – our destiny. We are not machines bound by some preordained programming that is unchangeable and out of our control.

There are certainly some things that are dictated by our genes. It is very unlikely that I will – by force of will – be able to change my eye colour or the shape of my ears. However, we know that eye colour does alter and change. We know of people who suffer with multiple personality disorder whose physical bodies alter completely when one of the different personalities comes to the fore. This can even be to the extreme of one personality being allergic to certain foods and the other one not! What does this tell us about the power of our beliefs about who we truly are to alter not only our thinking and behaviour but the actual chemical and physical composition of our bodies? And this can be extended to the brain as well.

Looking at the relatively new field of neuroplasticity, once again we have been proven wrong after scientists and physicians believed for decades that the physical makeup, structure and function of the brain was set in stone. The prevailing belief has always been that if one part of the brain is damaged there is no recovering or regeneration. However, one read through Norman Doidge's *The Brain that Changes Itself* shows us very quickly the amazing capacity of our brains to adapt and how one part of the brain can effectively take over what was once thought to be the sole domain of another part of the brain. We are also just beginning to understand that it is not true that brain cells, once destroyed, can never be replaced by new cells.

We truly do not understand the immense capacity of the brain and body to heal, repair and overcome any disease process or disability.

I would like to thank and acknowledge my good friend Mr. Rael Cohen for forwarding this next piece of information only recently as I was writing this chapter.

Dr. Daniel Amen, a psychiatrist who became fascinated with how the brain functions and the connection between damage to the brain and behavioural and psychological disturbances, gave a Ted X talk in 2013.

During his speech he described how brain spectral imaging had become a lost art and science when it came to the field of psychiatry. Here is a direct quote from his speech which has now had over 5.4 million views (I doubt very much many of those views were from psychiatrists questioning whether their methods of medicating anxiety and depression were efficacious and safe):

"Did you know that psychiatrists are the ONLY medical specialists that virtually never look at the organ they are treating?"

He described how when he was treating patients with medication in the past he couldn't help but feel like he was throwing darts at his patients in the dark…and hurting some of them quite badly. He went on to say that treatment needs to be tailored to each individual's brain and what is happening to them individually rather than to a "cluster of symptoms" which have been observed or reported to them and which appear to match a condition called depression, anxiety, OCD or any other mental health condition. And I say condition and not disorder because by its very nature a condition is temporary and can change over time. The injured person can heal over time with the right support, training, dietary and lifestyle changes. There is nothing fatal about having anxiety or depression. It only becomes fatal when others try to get the person to believe they cannot recover.

At the end of his Ted X speech, Dr. Amen says:

"After 22 years and looking at over 83,000 brain scans, the single most important lesson that we have learned is that you are not stuck with the brain you have; you can make it better and we can prove it."

There is an almost magical ability that we human beings possess when it comes to our capacity to heal ourselves through the right selection of thoughts, emotions, actions, lifestyle and experiences. We also know that our subconscious mind has the power to both elevate and heal our lives or to drag us down to the depths of despair. And something even more startling is the idea that some people seem to attract the very negative things they constantly think and talk about right into the life experience!

As far back as the 1960s, Dr. Joseph Murphy wrote what is now a classic book called *The Power of your Subconscious Mind* in which he details a number of cases where it was obvious to him that someone's habits of thinking and belief had led directly to physical and situational outcomes. These seemingly coincidental and "uncontrollable" events ended up being – as he observed - directly in line with what people believed to be true. Not what was true in "reality" but what became true in their reality when they gave enough energy to the thoughts and beliefs that they insisted on carrying around with them.

Everywhere we find evidence of the "self-fulfilling prophecy". It is worth pondering why such a saying even exists and why it has been around for so long. As Dr. Wayne Dyer was fond of saying, what you think about expands and if you contemplate a thing for long enough, give it enough energy and "airtime", so to speak, in your mind, there is a strong likelihood that the thing you think about is going to present itself to you in physical reality.

For example, I work with a lot of people who come into counselling complaining about how things keep going wrong for them. They recount each "injury" that people have done to them but it is not the injury itself but the ongoing mental attention to it that continues to impact their lives. There was one particular woman who came to see me who had been struggling to get her life on track for most of her adult life. She had never had a significant relationship, never married, never had kids, was in debt and hated her job. She was now in her mid-forties and during the first few sessions I let her vent and get all her frustration, disappointment and heartache off her chest. However, as the sessions progressed and I had provided her with the tools to identify her faulty and negative thoughts and beliefs and to dispute them, she just continued to spout the negativity to me in each session. They were extremely heavy sessions and I often found myself very drained afterwards because I was trying to give her positive energy to help her shift her thinking and belief system. Our first sessions came to a close and she promised to work on changing her thoughts and beliefs, even though she appeared to be very sceptical as to the connection between the results she was achieving in her life and her own thinking patterns.

About a year later, she booked in to see me again. She came in, sat down and I asked her how things were. And she began to describe a litany of events that had happened in the previous year that she said "proved" that the universe was conspiring against her. She said she was no closer to achieving any of the goals she had wanted to move towards the year before. So, I asked her whether she had been catching her negative thoughts and attempting to dispute them, to which she replied that she couldn't see the point because nothing would change anyway.

It seems that some people resolutely refuse to reflect on how thoughts are truly things and they are creative in our lives. A thought (positive or negative) has the power to lead us to our most cherished goals and desires in life and it has infinite power to stop us in our tracks, hold us back and prevent us from having what we want.

In many cases, the thing that we may want is the return of our physical or mental health and wellbeing. However, if we have the thought that we are completely governed by our genetics and that "there is a history of mental illness in my family", which means that we are genetically programmed to experience anxiety or depression, we are doing ourselves a major disservice. We are effectively abdicating any personal power or responsibility to change our lives. We can then hand over the reins and destiny for our mental and physical health to the "experts" - the medically trained scientists who we have all come to believe must hold the last word on truth and reality. Right?

However, as I said in the beginning, some of the greatest scientific minds that ever lived, including Albert Einstein and Max

Planck (who won the Nobel Prize for Physics in 1918), have shown us that there are things that occur in their research that just don't add up and do not confirm to what the original theories have been about the nature of reality and how things truly work and come to be in our universe.

Take, for example, spontaneous remission from cancer and in particular take the case of Anita Moorjani, who was diagnosed with lymphoma in February 2002 and after a four-year battle and even after several conventional cancer treatments went into a coma which by every account she should not have come out of. There was no coming back from the kind of cancer she had and the stage that it had led to within her body, with large "lemon-sized" tumours all over her upper body. The doctors told her family that her organs were shutting down and that she was in her final hours of life.

But Anita experienced what is referred to as an NDE (near death experience), and miraculously awoke knowing she would be healed and within four days, her tumours had shrunk by 70% and weeks later the cancer had completely left her body. Her book, *Dying to be me*, became a bestseller after Dr. Wayne Dyer hunted her down and asked her to write her story. She has written more books since her first and gives talks all over the world. All the facts of her case have been verified and checked; otherwise she would have been declared a fraud.

What Anita experienced and then managed to achieve defies scientific and medical theory, practice, thinking, understanding and process. She should have died. Not only did she come back from the coma, she came back to a complete healing from the cancer within a few weeks. How does science explain this?

More importantly, how does Anita explain this? I would suggest you read her book to find out but essentially, she ascribes her unbelievable case of spontaneous remission to experiencing what it was like to be free of her body and getting a glimpse of what her life story meant and finding compassion for herself as well those who had caused her the suffering and pain which she believes led to the cancer in the first place. She also described being greeted by her late father and a close friend when she went into the coma and that they told her it was not her time and that she should return and "live her life fearlessly".

Anita connects her cancer directly with her own negative belief system about herself and about her life and what it all meant. The NDE helped her to break free of the limiting beliefs – including the belief that cancer is incurable! – and come back to a full, vibrant and completely healthy life. She now lectures all over the world, bringing her message of hope to millions.

Now, I KNOW there are those of you who just read that and are very close to throwing this book across the room. And that's okay. But I ask you to just contemplate this because I believed even as you did that my experiences, biology and life path were all locked into place and that my chances of changing things around were slim. However, I always had some part of me that held onto the hope that I could create a miracle – or at least a miracle to me – of being able to get off antidepressants after 17 YEARS of being stuck on them.

Aside from the rare outlier I had come across, the majority of people who suffered with anxiety and depression and who had tried to get off antidepressants had been unable to. There are website support groups which discuss these terrible and heartbreaking physical and emotional withdrawal cases. However, after having connected with these types of groups I realised that all it was doing was hooking me deeper and deeper into the story of how impossible it was to get off antidepressants after so long. Some people had taken years to taper, cutting the tablets down to the tiniest percentages with Excel spreadsheets by 0.15mg, etc. I realised that what I needed to do as I tapered off was to completely remove my attention from the problem and focus only on the possibility of being free and living my life as me again.

I started creating the belief that what I cherished and desired more than anything in the world – to be free of antidepressants – was not only possible but that it was already underway. And I chose to look for any evidence at all in my body, mind and emotions that this was true. I created an affirmation which I placed in the reminders on my phone which popped up (and still does) every single morning which says "I AM perfect mental and physical health...and so it is" and that affirmation which I struggled so hard to even contemplate or look at sometimes has now – a few short years later - become my reality. The act of even contemplating the affirmation or allowing it to enter my mind consciously and then subconsciously – began to change what I thought and in turn what I did when it came to my health and wellbeing. We have to turn away from negative and potentially self-fulfilling prophesies about who we are and what we are. If we are going to continue to affirm and believe *anything* why not let it be something that will be helpful to us? Why not choose thoughts and affirmations which will lead us in the direction of that which we want as opposed to what we fear or do not want in our lives?

Dr. Wayne Dyer himself was diagnosed with leukaemia at the age of 69 but completely refused to follow modern medical treatments. He writes about his journey in his book *Wishes Fulfilled*. When he passed away six years later at the age of 75, the autopsy revealed no trace of cancer in his body. Louise Hay healed herself of cancer through natural methods thirty years before that. People do it everyday and it is referred to as "spontaneous remission". However, there is nothing spontaneous about it. These anomalies come about from an amazingly deliberate and sometimes very stubborn human being who uses his or her belief in something infinitely more powerful than a medical test to decide when their time on earth will come to an end.

Science cannot explain the experiences of Anita, Wayne and Louise or the hundreds and thousands of human beings who defy the odds and recover from the most difficult and sometimes deadly diagnoses.

I certainly don't place my own experience with anxiety, depression and being told that I needed to stay on antidepressants for life in the same category as theirs; however, what I have achieved was not meant to be possible either. Remember, people with anxiety and depression have "chemical imbalances" that can only be corrected effectively by taking "medications", just like a diabetic needs insulin for the rest of their life. Unfortunately, due to the withdrawal syndrome that most people get stuck on when trying to come off these drugs, most of them probably will be on the drugs for life. And the quality of their lives will be severely limited and compromised by the very drugs that are meant to be making them happier.

Maybe one day science will be able to explain the outliers and anomalies who don't accept that there is only one reality and one truth in the world. For now, we need to realise that having a mind that is open to everything and attached to nothing (which was one of Dr. Dyer's 10 secrets for success and inner peace) is truly one of the wisest ways to live our lives.

CHAPTER NINE

Finding your passion again

"Find your passion, whatever it may be. Become it and let it become you and you will find great thing happen for you, to you and because of you"

- T. Alan Armstrong

There is nothing more powerful than something that moves your spirit. When we are born, there are things that we navigate to in this life through our own very natural preferences. These desires are born with us. No one can really explain what moved a Mozart at the age of four or five to write a symphony or a Michelangelo to paint the Sistine chapel, or a Steve Jobs to create Apple. But it doesn't matter what it is that moves you, what matters is that you don't ever let it stop moving you. Not for anything or anyone. Because your life may depend on it one day.

For some people it's cooking, for some people its painting, for others it's dancing and for others it may be sport or another hobby. For me, it has always been and always will be music and singing. I also love reading and writing; however they don't move me the same way music does.

So, I know when depression is trying to take me on because that is usually the exact moment when I find myself unable to listen to music. It's one thing to choose to not do the things that give you the greatest joy in life, but it's a completely different experience to have it taken away from you by depression. The thing about depression is that it will rob you of the ability to enjoy the very things that make life worth living. And that becomes a terrible trap of despair that you absolutely HAVE to beat.

Do not let depression dictate whether you are going to live or die or whether you are going to enjoy your life every day.

Anxiety and depression are the ultimate dark magicians; they can make you see your life in a completely different way to the way it is in reality. And believe me, you will think it's real. You will think that the thoughts you are having are the truth and reality of your life. But they just aren't. When you are stuck in a depressive state, the thoughts you have are completely different to the thoughts you would have if you were feeling better. It is a catch-22 that you need to feel better before you can begin to think differently about your life and you need to think differently in order to start to feel better about your life. So my challenge to you is this: What can you do right now, in this moment, that will shift your mental and emotional state towards something even slightly better? Do you need to call a friend? Do you need to get out of the house and go for a walk in nature? Do you need to get out of that bed and run your ass off until you can't breathe and the sweat is pouring off you? Then go and do it. Go now.

Hear me now: YOU are the only one who is going to change this. Yes, you may need some moral support—a counsellor, a friend, a family member, a work colleague, or anyone to support you along the way—but make no mistake...only YOU are going to change this around and take your life back.

One of the things that may work in your bag of tricks against anxiety and depression may very well be the hobbies and passions you have allowed to slip away.

You may have reasons why you let yourself stop dreaming, why you allowed yourself to stop doing those things that give you the most joy in your life. But let me tell you, there is no reason on this earth for you to stop doing the things that bring you joy and that connect your spirit to the world. You know what those things are and if you don't, think back to your childhood or your teen years. What were you naturally drawn to do? What did you dream of doing one day in your life? Sing, dance, perform, build, create, share, connect, help, save others? There is nothing stopping you from doing these things right now, only your beliefs about why you think you cannot do them.

Yes, you may be stuck in the throes of a depressive state; believe me, no one understands that better than I do. But I also know something else that you may not know. I know the other side of it. I know the joy you can find on the other side, and you know something? The other side can be just a moment away...a decision away, a word away, a book away, or a conversation away.

You can and you will come back from this. You need to get yourself into the mindset that I had to get myself into, which is the mindset of NEVER GIVING UP. EVER! THAT, my friends, is the Black Belt Mind in action. You will never develop a black belt mind if you choose to give up. So, you may as well reach for it and keep going. I became a black belt in Tae Kwon Do under one of the toughest Tae Kwon Do masters in the world. I didn't do it by becoming discouraged when I felt like I was a failure compared to all the others who seemed to have progressed so much quicker than me. I didn't do it because I have some special talent that you don't. I did it by deciding that I would continue on and that I would just see where life took me. I got to a point where I wanted to quit very close to become a black belt because of how difficult it had been studying psychology for five years whilst doing three Tae Kwon Do classes every single week. I had a conversation with my Tae Kwon Do master telling him that I was going to leave. And let me tell you, he didn't take it well! It gave me pause to reflect on what he said, some of which was overly harsh but mostly helpful and helped to push me further to achieve the black belt I had worked so hard towards for the previous six years. I had to say to myself that I would not be the one to tap out. I would continue to learn, to grow, to feel the ups and downs and eventually I reached the goal of becoming a black belt in Tae Kwon Do and the prize of achieving a goal I didn't think I would achieve.

And you know what? That milestone was just a first step on my journey to developing a black belt mind. It was nothing compared to what I then endured over the next seventeen years after being prescribed antidepressants for anxiety at the age of twenty-four.

As I was saying before, one of the hardest parts of getting stuck in depression is not being able to enjoy your passions and allowing yourself to be elevated by them. Our passions ignite our energy and help reconnect us to meaning and show us that we still have a beautiful and deeply meaningful life to experience. As Max Erhmann said in Desiderata, "With all its sham, drudgery and broken dreams, it is still a beautiful world". Not only is it a beautiful world, it is *your* beautiful world because what you choose to observe each day and what *you* choose to focus on and enjoy is totally up to you.

Remember: "Failure cannot cope with persistence"—and neither can anxiety or depression. I promise you that. So, stick to it and engage with those passions again. There are passionate people all around you who will be there to help you find your passions again. Stop looking down and just lift your head up a little. You will see them standing right there, waiting for you to take a step. And if you can't take a step (sometimes literally), they will still be there to lift you up. But it requires at least the will from you to keep trying. There is nothing on this earth more powerful than your faith and hope that "this too shall pass" to break anxiety and depression. And as you begin to engage with the passions that you loved before, you start to feel better, and those passions will help energise and motivate you even more and you will remember why it is that you love this life and how much more you still want to live and experience it all.

Write down some of the things in life which bring you the greatest thrill and which speak to your soul. These are things you have been drawn to most of your life and that you just love to do. Write them down below and then go and do any one of them. Even if it's just for ten minutes. Go and live your life and remember that a reawakening of your joy and power is just an action away, taken each day.

1. _____

2. _____

3. _____

4. _____

CHAPTER TEN

What you resist will persist

"You cannot continue to keep alive within you vibrational patterns of what you do not want and expect to receive what you do want"

– Esther Hicks

You have to release the story of who you have been up to now and move forward into another concept of who you are becoming.

One of the most important keys to doing this is to stop talking about it. Stop blogging about it; stop trying to convince other people that change needs to happen or that you don't need it anymore. There is a very powerful quote which says, "Tell the world what you want to achieve, but show it first". You might like to apply that to yourself! Don't even keep talking to yourself about what you are going to do. Just do it. Every day.

Whenever you tell others around you about your intentions to change anything or to achieve anything in your life, you are not likely to get the reaction that you were hoping for. Most people think they will get support, encouragement and motivation from those they love and who are closest to them when they want to change their lives around. Unfortunately, that is very seldom the case in reality.

If you want to achieve something great, something daring, something that most people couldn't even think of achieving and then you go and tell those people what you want to do, you are only going to invoke their ego. Their ego will not like the fact that you are attempting to do something extraordinary. This may be because they have seldom – if ever - attempted anything like that in their own lives and you will just be a constant reminder to them of that fact. And so, what do you think they are most likely to do, whether it is conscious or subconscious? They will attempt to dissuade you from taking action. They will tell you all the reasons why you cannot become the person you want to be because of who you have been in the past. They don't want their concept of you to change. They may have subconsciously been perfectly fine with you struggling and being stuck and dependent on them. You changing would force them to re-conceive their evaluation and opinion of who you are and most people are too lazy and self-centred to do that. They prefer that their conception of the world remains stable.

How dare you go from being anxious, depressed and broke to being joyful, vibrantly healthy and rich! That just doesn't compute for them because that would mean that they were wrong about you all along. So which one is the *real* you? Well, in the end, it doesn't matter who they think the real you is. It only matters who *you* think the real you is. Whatever your belief is about who you are and what you can be, do or have is the most important opinion.

Other people's doubts, negativity and put-downs can be a very powerful force which can stop you right in your tracks. But if you are aware that this is likely to happen and to come from those who are supposedly closest to you and who are meant to care about your wellbeing and success, then you can take steps to protect yourself against their likely responses.

Decide right now, in this moment, that any changes that you wish to make in your life to turn things around for the better should be kept very private to you and only entrusted to those you absolutely know who will support you 150% in making the changes you wish to make.

Another reason it is better not to tell people what you want to do or even to discuss your issue that you are trying to overcome is because every time you talk about it, write about it or engage with it you are giving over energy to the problem and making it bigger.

Stop activating what you don't want anymore.

The more you push against something the stronger it becomes. As the saying goes, "what we resist persists" – which is amazingly true.

There are times when you need to stand up and fight. Not push back but fight. And what I mean by this is to intelligently apply your mental and physical energy toward resolving or overcoming a life issue. I am certainly not saying that you should become aggressive or a bully. I am only saying that there is a time for good people to fight back and overcome the enemy. There is a time for good people to take a stand and say "no more". This could apply to any arena in life. The hardest part is knowing when to let go and stop resisting something and to change your point of focus and therefore allow the issue to dissolve on its own due to your lack of attention to it and knowing when to stand up to a person or situation and remove it/them from your life.

Giving your mental and/or physical energy towards trying to fight against your anxiety and depression will only give it more power over you.

One day in February 2018, after proving to myself that I could do things that I didn't really believe I could do (like getting up every morning at 5:00 and running 5kms), I was staring at a box of Prozac that had been sitting in its usual place on the shelf. A strange thought- sensation came over me – almost like a sense of a defining moment – you know those ones where you know that something that just happened or is about to happen is probably going to be a defining moment in your life and be imprinted on your memory forever?

My relationship to antidepressants had begun to shift and change in the sense that I no longer felt animosity towards them. For so many years, I had an oppositional stance when it came to the antidepressants. To be honest, I really hated them and the fact that I just couldn't seem to get off them, no matter how hard I tried, how much research I did, or how slowly I tapered.

However, I did know that I had been successful in coming off them in the past, most notably in 2013, when I successfully weaned myself off Prozac. As I mentioned before, I remained off the antidepressants for six months but unfortunately two major life upheavals occurred very soon after I stopped taking them and I was just not prepared enough to cope with the challenge of that level of stress on my system so soon after coming completely off the antidepressants. I ended up back on them in January 2014 and my life became hell for the next four years. I wrote about having to go back on antidepressants in a follow-up article for Mad in America because I ended up writing to Robert Whitaker after I started to receive so many emails from people all over the world asking me for help – but I felt like a fraud having ended up back on them. I actually asked Robert to take my article down but he said rather than that to write a follow-up story because my experience was not unique and people needed to know they were not alone in this epic battle to get off the antidepressants. And so I did. And now part three is available on the Mad in America site, which I very purposely timed to coincide with the release of this book to show people that it may have taken another few years of research, of painful experience and debilitating situations, but I finally did it.

And so it was in February 2018, after I had begun to make major changes to my diet, my thinking, my beliefs and my physical activity (including my 5am runs as well as practicing Tae Kwon Do once more), I found myself looking at the box of Prozac and having an interesting conversation with it in my mind.

The monologue went something like this:

"I think it is time we had a talk. We've been together for a long time now. We have had a lot of ups and downs. I know that I have a fear of what life would be like without you and I don't have any guarantees that I can make it out there on my own...but to stay with you is not the answer either.

I appreciate everything you have tried to offer me, which included blunting my pain and my real emotions. I know your purpose in doing that was to "protect" me so I didn't feel the pain and so that I can get on with my life. But I fear the price I have paid for your concern and your desire to 'save' me has been much more than the benefits you have given me. You have given with one hand just as you took away with the other.

It has taken me a very long time to understand you. I wish I had known earlier or figured it out earlier. I certainly wasn't warned about you.

When we first met and before we got to know each other, everyone was very positive about you and they all thought we should be together forever and that we were 'made for' each other.

However, I now see that whilst you may have been made for me, I was never made for you. The truth is, you were made for everyone and I was just one of the millions who fell into your trap.

I have come to realise that being in a relationship where there is more taking than giving is never going to end well. Someone is going to get hurt, badly. And I know it won't be you, because you have your sights set on so many others and if you aren't trying to destroy me, you will just move on to destroying the next poor sap who isn't warned to stay away from you.

And so, I think it is time that you and I break up. I will give you some time to get your things together and leave completely but I am putting you on notice as from today. Your days are numbered. I have come to realise that I deserve something better. You promised me the world and you delivered only pain and suffering.

As hard as it will be to let you go, I have made up my mind. I do thank you for being in my life because without you, I would never have learned who I truly am. I would never have learned how powerful and undefeatable my spirit is. I would never have learned who my real friends are, nor for that matter who would truly stick by me through thick and thin.

And so what you have actually brought to my life was a very sharp divide and incredibly clear distinction between those I can truly call my "family" here on Earth and those who are only there by virtue of bloodlines or their own special interests.

You have taught me that self-reliance is critical to any human development and flourishing; you have also taught me the value of those who are selfless and how to differentiate between those who deserve my time, my love, my attention, my respect and my support and those who don't.

For all of the immeasurable benefits you have given me, I thank you.

For all of the immeasurable damage you have done in my life, I forgive you.

It wasn't your fault, after all. You could only play out your intended purpose in my life and nothing more. And now it is time for me to play out my intended purpose in this lifetime...without you.

So, this is goodbye...we shall not meet again unless through your association with others who may come to me for advice about how to let you go. Because in the end, you can't change who or what you are...but I most certainly can."

And that was the last time I took an antidepressant and I have not looked back and I also know that no matter what the future holds for me, there is nothing that would ever lead me back down that road because as Esther Hicks is fond of saying, I know too much and there is no turning back.

Learning to turn your focus away from the thing that you fear and face towards the things that you actually do want is something I think was a critical part of my success. And I think it is also a very powerful analogy for just about any other thing that you may be stuck on and which is causing you pain and difficulty in your life.

Decide that you will now begin to focus on what you want. If what you want is joy, peace and happiness then look for things that are the most likely to give you those feelings and experiences. If what you want is financial stability and abundance then start to focus on what will give you the greatest feeling that you are indeed heading in that direction. Maybe it means getting a job, maybe it means changing your job or career or maybe it means you need to start learning about finance and how to grow your money through becoming an investor. I promise you one thing: if you begin to focus your attention on the things that you want and which are exciting, enjoyable and growth-compelling for you, it won't be long before you turn around and see that you have come miles and miles from where you thought you were so stuck and you cannot even remember what it feels like to be in that place anymore.

And finally, when you do succeed, don't ever forget what it felt like when you were down there in the trenches because someone, somewhere is going to need your help one day and you will need to find that space inside you that remembers what it was like to be where they are now so that you can show them the way out.

CHAPTER ELEVEN

You are not who you think you are...

"The Tao that can be named is not the Tao"

- Lao Tzu

During one particular conversation with my Tae Kwon Do master, we got onto speaking about the different words, names or labels that are used by humans to try and classify something. From my studies in psychology and especially cognitive psychology, I had learned that the human brain likes to categorise things. It makes for a more efficient way of being in the world. We generalise, stereotype and classify everything from plants to our fellow human beings, as this is a simpler way to manage all the information that comes at us every day.

For example, if I have had an interaction with a fellow human being who is not the same ethnicity to me or maybe there are religious, cultural or any other "differences", my brain may create some simple ways of coding and then classifying that interaction with "that kind of person". We do this so that when we come across that person or that "type of person" again in the future we can immediately reference some information about them, which we think saves us some time in knowing who or what we are dealing with.

This may seem logical and efficient; however, it is perilously unhelpful in managing our interactions with the world around us. Why? Because it is a fallible system which is filled with incomplete pieces of information and anecdotal evidence which we often fail to verify or go into greater detail with because we are inherently lazy when it comes to trying to understand the world around us. Through this way of classifying the world, but more importantly this way of classifying not only others but ourselves, we have made a huge mistake in understanding the depths of the person we are looking at. Including that person we look at in the mirror every morning.

We completely underestimate ourselves and have often been told during the course of our lifetime by those well-meaning and sometimes not so well-meaning influential people (parents, teachers, friends, peers, colleagues, etc.) who we are, what our limitations are, what our weaknesses are, what our strengths are, what our capabilities are, and even what our POTENTIAL is. The latter is so critical to the understanding of this book and what its message is that I want you to really take note.

No-one knows what your true potential is. No-one truly understands who you really are and what you are capable of achieving. Not even YOU. How could you possibly know given everything you have been told and everything you have lived in your life…until now.

Sounds horribly fatalistic and sad, doesn't it? You don't even know what you are capable of. But the wonderful truth of this is…

YOU HAVE NO IDEA WHAT YOU ARE TRULY CAPABLE OF!

And that means you will have to wipe out everything you think you know about yourself and then go ahead and try something new, something different, something you have always wanted to, something you have always dreamed of doing, something your heart calls out to you to do.

It is only in every moment, every NOW that you have your "point of power", as the wonderful Louise Hay used say. This means you have no power in your past and you have no power in your future to act and change the direction of your life. Your only power is right here and now in what you decide to do next.

And along with that are the barriers that have been set up by others and yourself in your own conscious and mostly subconscious minds about who you are and what you are allowed to be do and have in this lifetime. All based on what? Someone else's misguided opinion.

After a particularly difficult conversation with my Tae Kwon Do master, I reflected overnight on what he had said to me about different categories of people such as "Europeans" as opposed to the "non-European" populations who he said were more genuine and open to others in general. I found his line of reasoning particularly difficult to absorb and so after giving it much thought as well as a good deal of subconscious processing, I awoke at 4am one morning and wrote the following message to him:

"Remember you said last night: when someone says to you, you are not God, you say how do you know? Have you met him or seen him? I agree 100% with that statement because in fact my conception of 'God' is that you can call him/her/it whatever you like; you can call it Buddha, God, Jesus, Louise, Tree, Source, Infinite intelligence, All-That-Is—it really doesn't matter what you call it because it just IS".

Lao Tzu (the famous Chinese philosopher), who wrote one of the most cherished texts on spiritualty called the Tao Te Ching around 300 BC, said "The Tao that can be named is not the Tao."

As soon as we try to name or label something we immediately lose its essence because labels are terribly useless at defining something, just as a name does not define anything. Jewish, Christian, Muslim, Black, White, David, Carrot, Idiot... you get the point.

Soren Kierkegaard wrote, "Once you label me, you negate me." Once you call me something, you don't really see me anymore. You only see your label because it makes life easier to put things or people into categories.

No human being on this planet will ever get wet by just reading or trying to understand the word 'water'. Without the experience of something, we will only ever have an 'intellectual or philosophical' understanding but never a knowing. True power comes from knowing. Not believing.

So, what we need to do, said Wayne Dyer, is move from a belief to a knowing. You need to move beyond your belief in all the labels that you have been given since you were born into a knowing about who you truly are and what you can be, do or have in this lifetime while you are here.

Those labels might be, for you and millions of others across the world, things like being stupid, lazy, inferior, unattractive, poor, sick, unwell, disordered etc.

Taking it one step further and moving now into the field of psychiatric "classification", we come to the bible of categorisation, labelling, and stereotyping: The Diagnostic and Statistical Manual or the DSM as it is known. This manual will give you a classification that allows you to be provided with government benefits in the United States while it brands you for life with a broad brush and some of the worst legally accepted ways of herding human beings into ill-defined and unscientific categories.

It will take away your uniqueness as a human being on this planet. It will take away your ability to define your own life and chart your own course in this life, free of the bondage of being prejudged, boxed, labelled and often (in the case of those who have been 'sectioned' in psychiatric hospitals or mental health wards) subjected to some of the most heinous 'treatments' around on the planet today outside of prisoner of war torture camps.

One of these "treatments" which incredibly still continues to be used behind the closed and locked doors of these psychiatric prisons of the human spirit are things like electroconvulsive 'therapy' (ECT), which involves hooking the brains of human beings - one of the most delicate and intricate organisms that exists on the planet - up to electrical points and frying them in the name of healing depression, bi-polar, schizophrenia and any other classifications the psychiatrists deem suitable for this most barbaric treatment of human beings.

And then there was the frontal lobotomy, the surgical severing of one of the most highly developed parts of the human brain from the more primal part, which was eventually frowned upon but was still used until only a few decades ago. Prior to this, psychiatrists would also do things like inject insulin into the body of patients and induce a seizure which would put the patient into a coma in order to "help" them with the mental health difficulties they were experiencing.

There are many excellent books written around this subject. If you do want to learn more about it I would suggest starting with one of the best authorities and authors, Dr. Peter Breggin – a psychiatrist himself, who has been a vocal opponent of some of the psychiatric treatments in the United States for decades.

The point I am trying to make here is that labels are dangerous.

From some of the simplest labels such as intelligent, smart, idiot, drop-out, jock, and nerd to the psychiatric classifications listed by the latest version of the DSM.

A fascinating read and account of this insanity of labelling difficulties that we as human beings struggle with as disorders which need classification and, in many cases, drugging is a book written by Dr. Allen Frances called Saving Normal.

Dr. Frances presided over the development and launch of the DSM-IV and after successfully completing this great undertaking by the American Psychiatric Association, he retired to spend some time with his grandchildren.

He kept abreast of the developments with the DSM from afar until he was invited as an 'alumnus' to a cocktail party launch of the project team that would head up the reinvention of the DSM and creating its next iteration...the DSM-V.

At that cocktail party, Dr. Frances was so shocked and eventually outraged at the number of new conditions, mental illnesses and categories that the team was gloating over that he came out of retirement to protest the development of the next DSM.

He identified that the direction in which psychiatry was heading was nothing short of appalling and was going to lead to the globalisation of everything human into a disorder to be classified and identified as being a mental health condition requiring some form of treatment.

If someone from within the psychiatric ranks who presided over one of the largest redevelopments of their bible can come out of retirement because he was so concerned, and risk his own professional standing to point out that the emperor had no clothes and that they were going down a very dangerous road of classifying every human experience and emotion as a disorder, then we should all be taking notice and asking critical questions about the classification of human beings into little boxes. Little boxes that can and do have tragic outcomes for those who are identified as falling into one of them.

We may find very soon that laziness is categorised as a mental health condition requiring mind altering drugs which may have lifelong consequences for someone's mental, physical, emotional and most importantly spiritual experience of what it means to be alive on this planet.

Whilst I do not deny that there is sometimes a need and a place for identifying what someone is suffering with, especially when it comes to severe disorders of the mind such as schizophrenia and other psychotic disorders, I believe we can and do go too far with labelling human beings. This is especially when it comes to anxiety and depression and the subsequent ongoing drugging of humanity with little or no follow up, support or encouragement to eventually wean off these drugs when it is desirable and possible to do so.

CHAPTER TWELVE

Question everything...and everyone

"The most important thing is to not stop questioning"

-Albert Einstein

Some truths are undeniable, such as the fact that the sun is shining today. I can try to convince myself that the sun in fact is not shining and that if I sit on the beach today at midday, close my eyes and fervently disbelieve that the sun is shining I will not get sunburned. That is a one-way trip not only to the burn clinic but to the men in white coats. (Sorry, couldn't resist).

Having said that, scientists are beginning to realise that there are things that they simply cannot explain about the very fabric and nature of "reality" as we know it.

Ultimately, in order to truly change your life, overcome stress, anxiety, or depression and to take a major leap for those of you who are trying to reclaim your lives from antidepressant drugs, you simply have to disregard everybody else's truth and start to believe in and trust your own intellect, instincts, physiology, and beliefs about who you truly are.

This is where the power of questions comes into its own. Nothing created by mankind in this world would ever have come into being if there wasn't first a question.

Can you imagine what the world would be like today if primitive man hadn't had a question swimming around in his brain which asked: "I wonder what will happen if I keep rubbing these two sticks together?"

What if Thomas Edison hadn't asked himself over a thousand times how he could create an electric incandescent light bulb?

What if the Wright brothers hadn't contemplated the possibility of humans flying in machines across the sky? It would take a long time to get from Los Angeles to Sydney, that's for sure.

And so, it is with even the simplest of questions in our own lives. Asking ourselves the right kinds of questions is critical to our own wellbeing, growth and development as human beings.

Those who don't ask any questions are doomed to stay stuck in the past and in repeat mode. It seems, however, that complacency is acceptable to a fairly large number of human beings. This certainly doesn't mean that you need to be one of them. In fact, if you truly want to change your life, you absolutely have to *keep* asking questions. The day my Tae Kwon Do master told me that I asked too many two-dollar flea market questions, I realised I was no longer dealing with a true master of life. This spelled the beginning of the end of our connection; even though he had seemed to reappear in my life almost miraculously and had helped kicked things into high gear for me at a pivotal moment. After fourteen years of first thinking he was dead and then reconnecting with him in the most unusual and somewhat cosmic way, the relationship came to a cataclysmic ending. I realised that anyone who tries to prevent anyone else from asking intelligent and completely relevant questions has something to hide or has such a large ego that they cannot stand needing to question their own thinking, assumptions or philosophy about life.

Remaining open and flexible to changing what you believe about life and, in particular, what you believe most deeply about yourself is critical to overcoming anxiety and depression – or just about anything else that you may find causing you difficulty.

Question EVERYONE

If people such as Oskar Schindler hadn't questioned the supreme authority of a monster such as Adolf Hitler, 1200 Jews would never have made it out of Germany alive.

If Marconi hadn't wondered if information could be transmitted directly through the air surrounding us, the world as we know it today would not exist in its current form.

Everyone has an opinion based on their own life experience and their own beliefs, biases and very often misconceptions that they have carried along with them – sometimes for a lifetime.

And so, we all need to think very carefully from whom we should seek advice. As Robert Kiyosaki would say, people who drive up to a financial planning meeting in a Rolls Royce generally don't take advice from people who come to work on the subway. Look for your guidance from those who have not only walked the path you are walking but also from those who have managed to move along that path to higher ground and who have the advantage of hindsight as well as foresight.

Going to a doctor who sits in front of you with a large belly for advice on how to lose weight is tantamount to going to a casino and asking the people surrounding the black jack table how to quit gambling. Probably a silly example, or is it? Maybe subtler than that example is when people go see a medical "expert" and listen very intently to their advice without ever asking them if they have any actual experience with the issue they are advising on in their own lives. PLEASE NOTE: I am absolutely *not* saying that this is a prerequisite for someone to have knowledge or some expertise in a particular profession or discipline; however, I am saying that with certain life experiences there is something missing from the knowledge and advice of those who have not walked down the path you are walking down. There always will be. They may have a belief but they can never have a knowing.

I know of parents who decided that before giving mind altering drugs to their children for diagnosed conditions such as ADHD, the would take the drugs – such as Ritalin - themselves first to experience exactly what would happen. When their experience shocked them to their very core about just exactly what the drugs did to their minds and their bodies they simply refused to give them to their children and looked for alternatives. They had developed a knowing, not a belief or theoretical understanding, about what the drugs could do to their children.

Throughout human history it seems it is always those who have dared to ask the hardest questions who have ended up contributing the greatest to our collective experience of life on earth. Questions like: "I wonder what would happen if...?" or "Why does it have to be this way?" "Who said that it must be this way?" "What are they getting out of this?" "Why do I still suffer so badly with depression when I am taking an *anti-depressant*?"

So, here is your turn to answer some important questions and you may want to sit right now and write down a few of your own:

- What have I learned so far from this book that I am absolutely determined to implement in my life?
- What am I going to start doing as of today?
- What am I going to stop doing?
- What have I not tried with a measure of discipline yet to beat anxiety and depression out of my life?
- What is holding me back from being disciplined and what can I do about it?

Keep asking the right questions and keep looking for answers and you will find your way out.

It can be no other way.

CHAPTER THIRTEEN

Hope: The last bastion of the human spirit

"There was never a night or a problem that could defeat sunrise or hope"

- Bernard Williams

Being a psychologist and very well-versed in the signs and symptoms of depression, I am very aware that one of the greatest mental difficulties that people with severe and debilitating depression experience is the loss of hope.

It is when people get down to that place where they feel hopeless, helpless and worthless that thoughts about ending it all may begin to rumble. When someone is in that state of mind, it is extremely difficult for them to realise that what they are thinking and feeling is not actually an objective or true reflection of what is happening in their lives. However, to the severely depressed person, this IS THE ONLY REALITY, and it is so painful both mentally and emotionally and has been going on for so long that they just want relief. They just want to feel their old selves again. In my case, after coming through the anxiety and depression and finally getting off the antidepressants, I actually felt like a completely different (but not unfamiliar) self because I also reconnected with who I was before all of it began.

There are a whole raft of thoughts and emotions that come with being in a depressed state of mind, not the least of which are the thoughts and feelings of being a burden to those they care the most about. People experiencing severe levels of depression will actually believe that their loved ones would be better off without them. They don't seem to have the ability to realise the incredible and irreversible pain that will be caused should they choose to take their own lives.

Fortunately, we know that getting suicidal people to see that they are not a burden and that those who love them would miss them terribly. This can often be the one thing that turns the tide or gets them to realise that suicide is not a solution. I have always liked the phrase that suicide is a permanent solution to a temporary human problem or condition.

Another useful analogy that can be put forward to those who are struggling is: Even nature cannot create a storm that is powerful enough to last forever. Eventually the storm passes, the clouds dissipate and the sun begins to peek through.

One of the absolutely crucial and life-saving human states of mind that needs to be cultivated in the mind of those who are severely depressed and who feel like they cannot conceptualise how things could ever get better, is HOPE. The state of mind and being that we experience as hope is the one thing that can start someone moving in the right direction and away from thoughts of ending it all.

For those who have found themselves stuck on antidepressant medications, this loss of hope can be even further reaching and debilitating. When a person feels that their life's direction is now at the mercy of a "chemical imbalance" or a reliance on drugs that are causing them sometimes unbearable side effects, one can begin to imagine the depths of despair these souls can have. I know because

I was one of them. But it was hope of recovery that always buffered me during those terrible times. It was that tiny glimmer of light inside that kept telling there was a way, that others had done it before me and that if I kept looking for answers and I just kept trying, I would succeed.

I am not saying I experienced despair that much – although there were certainly many times when I did – however, I fully appreciate and empathise with those who have been trying in vain to get off the "medications" that were meant to have helped them, but which have now become the jailor to their soul.

And so, what is to be done for those who are feeling trapped? What answer is there for those who have been beaten down by anxiety and depression again and again? What could possibly help save them and get them inching their way back to the surface where the air is clear, the water is crisp and the warm and life-giving sunlight can be felt on their faces?

HOPE.

What a strange little word that is. Four letters that join together and sit there on the page like just any other word and I suppose we can all be forgiven for reading it and just moving on. We could be forgiven for looking at that word and not really engaging with its meaning or the power that word has to save people's lives. To save *your* life or someone you intimately know and love. Yes, I am talking to you, reader. This is where we get personal. This is where I want to connect with your mind right now. Stephen King wrote in his autobiographical book *On Writing* that he believes that the art of writing is also, in fact, a form of time travel. I am writing these words to you right now on July 13, 2018 at 7:55am. You may be reading these words six months from now, a year from now or even ten years from now. I don't know who you are, which country you live in, how old you are, what gender you are or what heritage you have...but right now, in this moment of time, I am time travelling and speaking to your mind directly through my thoughts and the words that I am communicating to you on this page. This is from me to you reading this book right now, so listen up closely, pay attention because what I am about to say in the next few lines may just be the most important thing you will read in this book, or any book for that matter.

There is ALWAYS a chance to change your life. There is ALWAYS an answer to your trouble and you CAN and WILL get through this but you absolutely have to hold onto your HOPE.

You need to connect with stories of others who have been beaten down and come back stronger, better, happier and more successful than ever before. You have to look around you for anything and I mean ANYTHING that can bring you a sense of relief and a feeling of hope that things can get better for you. Because they can and they will if you make a promise to yourself and to me that you will NEVER, EVER GIVE UP.

Sure, you can stop for a while. Sure, you can recluse yourself to your bedroom, your cave, your mountain, your tent or your pillow for a while to recover, to meditate, to connect with your spirit and to remember who you really are, but you need to commit to yourself that no matter what goes before you, you will never be the one who pulls the plug on this life experience. Why? Because we need you. Because the people around you need you. And I don't just mean family or friends. I mean everyone who comes across your path needs you because that's why they have come across your path.

You don't know whose life you are going to touch and maybe even save.

Let me give you an example from my life a few years ago.

After I got divorced, I would always get my boys every Tuesday night and take them to school on a Wednesday morning. I decided that since I couldn't have quantity time with my boys, I would do everything I could to have quality time with them and so part of our weekly ritual was to go to a cake and pie shop called Michele's Patisserie before I dropped them at school every Wednesday morning. My boys would have a pie and I would have a coffee. Great healthy breakfast, I know but I wouldn't change it for the world. We have since moved onto healthier breakfasts. This became a very special time for us and we continued to do this for the next five years. During that time, we would sit at benches near the coffee shop and there was a little old lady who was always there at the same time every Wednesday morning. We would say hello every now and then and she would laugh and talk to my boys. She actually became very fond of them and seeing them every Wednesday morning and she watched with interest as they grew bigger and bigger.

Leah and I would talk on those Wednesday mornings and I found out she was Jewish and that she had escaped Nazi Germany as a child by being hidden by her mother in storm drains.

She took an interest in everyone around her who happened to come and sit down and have a coffee. She would wave or say hello to so many people it was like she owned the whole shopping centre. But she was just a beautiful soul who loved connecting to the people around her, people she didn't even know but came to know by just showing up at a coffee shop each morning.

Leah would ask me how I was when no one else bothered. She would see the pain in my eyes that others couldn't or wouldn't see and she would say something to me. She would share some of her own experience, she would make suggestions for taking something to help and more than anything she would try and give me hope that things would work out. There were many mornings when we sat there and my boys were eating their pies that she would ask how I was and the tears would just well up in my eyes. I didn't want the boys to see and so I had to get up and get a serviette from the counter, wipe my eyes and nose, compose myself and sit down again.

Leah gave me hope. She showed me that there are people out there who have compassion and love for others around them that is almost angelic. In fact, I feel that Leah was indeed an angel who appeared in my life out of nowhere for a reason. She didn't ask for anything other than a few minutes of conversation once a week and I supported her in whatever way I could when she would tell me of the physical problems that had been afflicting her. She was one of those people who just seem to come across our paths at our greatest hour of need and sometimes we just can't explain how that perfect timing works. We will often think back and say thank God that person seemed to appear at just the right time and in the strangest place.

Leah stopped appearing at the coffee shop a little while after that and I didn't have any contact details for her or chance to share with her how things improved and how I turned it all around. My boys and I often talk about her whenever we go for our morning coffee and hot chocolates. Told you we moved onto healthier breakfasts, right?

Leah appeared in my life and gave me hope to carry on, and then she was gone. She probably doesn't know how much it meant or the actual extent of what I was feeling at the time but she was one of the only ones who recognised it and showed the human courage to reach out to another human being and say it's okay, it's going to be alright.

Now it is my turn to say to you...*it is okay and everything is going to be alright!*

It is my turn to tell you to find your faith and your hope again and then you will start to find your joy creeping in again too.

And then it will be *your* turn to pass the hope and faith onto others who might need your help. Like I said earlier, we are all interdependent; no one stands alone and certainly no one thrives alone. We do need you as much as you need us, so don't ever give up.

EPILOGUE

Warning: The side effects of being off antidepressants

> *"The human spirit is more powerful than any drug. And that is what needs to be nourished. With work, play, and friendship. These are the things that matter. This is what we'd forgotten. The simplest things"*
>
> Robin Williams – *from the movie "Awakenings"*

I thought it would be worthwhile sharing in this last chapter a little of what has been happening for me since finally breaking free of anxiety, depression and antidepressants.

It has been such a fascinating journey and experience for me.

Going right back to the beginning of the book where I referenced some of the side effects of what people experience when they are going on antidepressants as well as all those horrible withdrawal effects, it would seem fair to try to describe the "side effects" of successfully coming off them.

Most people who have a desire to be free of these drugs are usually experiencing some distressing side effects being on them or other longer term, ongoing and sometimes very debilitating effects from being on them for so long just as I was. There are a lucky few who – when being prescribed antidepressants – tried them and had such bad physical reactions that they stopped taking them immediately and never bothered to see drugs as an option again. These people unwittingly dodged a bullet compared to those poor souls who struggle through the initial side effects - because they are told it takes six weeks for the drugs to work - and then...oh then...they are trapped.

Not everyone, of course, because some people seem to be able to get off them relatively easily but those people may have only been on them for a few months. However, this varies wildly according to each individual. You could take them for a few weeks and be stuck in withdrawal when you try to stop.

My experience has been quite hair-raising at times when I have come across some of the cases of the hundreds of people who have written to me from all over the world about what the antidepressants are doing to their minds, their bodies and their lives.

All their stories as well as my own have made me (fortunately or unfortunately) an expert in what antidepressant drugs can do to people with regards to some of the longer-term effects:

Just a few are:

- Akathisia (a loss of control of the muscles and nerves which is terribly painful and leads to involuntary arm and leg movements which are incredibly embarrassing and distressing);
- Blunted emotions (an inability to truly connect with what they are feeling about anything);
- Heart disease;
- Liver disease;
- Memory impairment;
- Loss of the ability to experience any pleasure from orgasm.

And those are just the physical effects. The impact on people's relationships, careers and family life is simply a tragedy that needs to be stopped.

When people are finally beginning to wean off antidepressant drugs with some success, they will often say things like:

"I feel like myself again"
"I can laugh again"
"I can cry again...but it's different kind of crying because it's a good crying; it's a release"
"My energy levels have increased"
"I'm enjoying my hobbies and interests again"
"I now remember who I used to be before the drugs" – this can be years or even decades later.
"My sex drive is back"
"I feel connected to the people around me again"
"I can't believe I was thinking and feeling all those terrible things"

I can certainly vouch for many of these. Having said that, everyone's experience of anxiety and depression as well as being on or off antidepressant drugs is highly unique to them. There are, however, undeniable consistencies and themes in people's stories. And I have heard enough of these stories directly from these people to have a complete appreciation for these consistencies in what people experience on and off these terrible drugs.

As devastating as the effects of an antidepressant tapering and withdrawal can be for people, it can be these little windows - where they are able to experience their true selves peeking through the dark clouds that have shrouded their minds for so long – that they begin to hang onto.

These people are all hanging onto hope, that little ray of hope that they so desperately need, which seems to whisper that they can indeed get back their minds, their relationships, their careers, their connection to their loved ones and their God-given right to live their lives the way they want to.

Getting down to basics however, there is something else at stake here which is so simple and powerful to everyone, no matter who they are or where they come from. And that is the simple fact that most of us just want to live peaceful, happy, loving, healthy and meaningful lives – free from disturbing external influences. And that is how it *should* be.

There are some simple life experiences that most people take for granted that can be taken away or at least severely muted to a large degree by these insidious drugs such as the taste of food, the touch of a loved one's hand, the delight at the moon shining brightly on a clear night, the ecstasy of music or movies that can move us all to tears, the absolute pleasure of being deeply physically and emotionally connected to our lovers, the sound of the waves crashing on the beach or the birds chirping merrily in the trees, or just the simple feeling of the bedsheets as we get into bed at night, and the comfort of our pillows. All these may seem like insignificant and everyday occurrences to most people.

But what I have come to know is that all of these experiences – which are part of the very "stuff" of life and what give this experience on Earth so much of its joy and meaning – are what so many of us take for granted. However, for those who are stuck in anxiety, depression or antidepressant withdrawal syndrome, these things become a focal point of pain and loss and sometimes a loss of hope that they will ever *feel normal* ever again. Losing that hope, as I said in the previous chapter, is sometimes fatal.

As some people come off the drugs successfully - due to being fully prepared physically, mentally, emotionally and spiritually for what comes next - they often discover that their anxiety and depression can be overcome and lifted. They discover the simple pleasures that start to return to be an unexpected and often bewildering and wonderful experience of *coming back to life.*

They begin to realise that they had been locked in a "pseudo-life" and that they had just been going through the motions of living life but they weren't truly feeling or staying connecting to it.

One of my clients recently expressed something to me that I could fully relate to. She was describing how she went to see a humorous children's movie with her two little girls and while everyone in the cinema was laughing and loving the movie, she just couldn't seem to access the humour in it. She knew on an intellectual level that it should be funny, but she couldn't laugh. I had a very similar and harrowing experience when I once took my kids to see an Alvin and the Chipmunks movie a few years ago. I was so locked up in a mental and emotional funk from the antidepressant that I just stared blankly at the ridiculously funny characters and felt a mixture of hopelessness, grief and bewilderment at my inability to enjoy such a simple pleasure and experience with my children. My client then said something quite eerie which made me stop and really reflect on just what these heinous drugs can do. She said: "It's like we've had a lobotomy".

And that is the very sad truth of all of this. These drugs may have some place in the world but I can't really come up with a place they actually have, to be honest. We really should be asking ultimately what all these millions of people - who have been placed on these drugs - are going through when it comes to the quality of their lives and what the impact is to their very existence as human beings.

Are we not meant to cry when something hurts? Are we not meant to grieve when someone we love goes away? Are we not meant to experience fear when we are under threat? Of course, fear and sadness that have become complicated and unrelenting need to be addressed through every means we have at our disposal. And there are plenty of options, as I hope my book has quite clearly shown you. There are so many things that we can try before we try antidepressants.

One of my favourite authors and speakers is Esther Hicks. She is fond of saying in her talks to her audiences: If the stove is hot and we put our hand on it, is not appropriate and necessary that our body signals pain to us so that we can take our hand off the hot stove? Or is it better to inject our hands with novocaine and then place our hands back on the stove and say: "Oh...that's much better. Doesn't hurt now...although I'm not sure I like that smell!"

No, my friends, we are not supposed to be numbed to our pain. It's a Band-Aid and as with a Band-Aid, taking it off may be painful but if we don't take it off we risk never being able to truly feel or enjoy life again as we used to or as we were meant to.

This was my experience too.

I'll never forget one of the first times I experienced a "reawakening" of my senses and my experience of life. I was driving with my now ex-wife and our kids back from a short holiday. I had been trying to taper off one of the drugs and had managed to get down to a very small fraction of a dose. As we were driving along, the sun suddenly broke from behind the clouds and shone on my forearm.

I got chills as I felt the warmth of the sun on my skin...as if I had never felt it before or more accurately, as I then realised I had not experienced having felt for the longest time. It was the most wonderful experience and it indicated to me in that moment that the antidepressants had been blocking something essential about my physical experience of life.

My experience has been on an even deeper and broader level this time around and I would even venture to say (at the risk of sounding like a madman) that it has been like a mental, emotional, physical and even spiritual reawakening. Having said that, if you were to ask anyone close to me who has seen me at my worst and who has walked this path with me at times, they would affirm the changes to you.

It is like, in some cases, people are meeting me for the first time, if they didn't know me before the antidepressants. It is like I am meeting myself, my real self again. And it has been a revelation that has led to my complete resolve that no matter what the future brings, and I mean *no matter what*, I will never again rely on anything but my own mind, body and spirit to heal anything that is causing me pain or discomfort in my life.

I am finally free...

Free to live my life as I choose.

Free to laugh.

Free to cry.

Free to grow.

Free to love.

Free to experience absolutely anything and everything this life has to offer me.

Most importantly, I am free to contribute my joy and hard-won knowledge to the world and to help all those who may be suffering and wondering if their experience of life will always be difficulty and pain and who may be wondering if their ability to enjoy a full and rich life has been tragically cut short.

I am here as living proof that that is not the case, that it doesn't have to be that way and that there is always hope of recovery and of finally overcoming anxiety, depression and antidepressants.

Further reading

Books regarding antidepressants

Toxic Psychiatry – Dr. Peter Breggin
Your drug may be your problem – Elliot Valenstein
Talking back to Prozac – Dr. Peter Breggin
Anatomy of an Epidemic – Robert Whitaker
Medication Madness – Dr. Peter Breggin
A mind of your own - Dr. Kelly Brogan
Saving Normal – Dr. Allen Frances
Prozac Backlash – Dr. Joseph Glenmullen
The antidepressant solution – Dr. Joseph Glenmullen

Self-Help: Psychology and Spirituality Books

There is a spiritual solution to every problem – Wayne Dyer
You can health your life – Louise Hay
The Law of Attraction – Esther and Jerry Hicks
Feeling Good: A New Mood Therapy – Dr. David Burns
Grain Brain – Dr. David Perlmutter

Websites
www.madinamerica.com
www.breggin.com
www.blackdoginstitute.org.au
www.reachout.com

ABOUT THE AUTHOR

David Fox is a psychologist, author, trainer and coach whose major professional driving force is to help others beat anxiety and depression. He is passionate about reducing the worldwide epidemic of the over-prescribing of antidepressant drugs which is becoming more widely acknowledged as a major worldwide health and well-being issue.

With a black belt in Tae Kwon Do, David uses his martial arts training as well as his deep knowledge and understanding of psychology and spirituality to help people transform their lives.

David is a corporate trainer and speaker who provides key-notes on the topic of mental health and is a passionate advocate of removing the stigma attached to discussing the difficulties that millions of people struggle with every day.

Connect with David:

Email: info@foxpsychology.com.au

Facebook: www.facebook.com/foxpsychology

Instagram: www.instagram.com/foxpsychology

Website & Blog: www.foxpsychology.com.au

David Fox

Black Belt Mind

www.ingramcontent.com/pod-product-compliance
Lightning Source LLC
Chambersburg PA
CBHW071916290426
44110CB00013B/1378